Fashion Doll Collection™ Book 3

General Information

Many of the products used in this pattern book can be purchased from local craft, fabric and variety stores, or from the Annie's Attic Needlecraft Catalog (see Customer Service information on page 63).

Ribbon Rose Gown DESIGN BY VAUNDA FISHER

SKILL LEVEL

INTERMEDIATE

FINISHED SIZE
Fits 11½-inch fashion doll

MATERIALS
- Size 10 crochet cotton: 200 yds white
- Size 8/1.50mm steel crochet hook or size needed to obtain gauge
- Sewing needle
- Matching sewing thread
- Small snaps: 2
- Ribbon roses: 5

GAUGE
9 dc = 1 inch; 9 dc rows = 1 inch

PATTERN NOTES
Join with slip stitch as indicated unless otherwise stated.

Chain-3 at beginning of row or round counts as first double crochet unless otherwise stated.

INSTRUCTIONS
GOWN
BODICE

Row 1: Beg at top, ch 45, dc in 4th ch from hook, dc in each ch across, turn. *(42 dc)*

Row 2: Ch 3 *(see Pattern Notes)*, dc in each of next 15 sts, 3 dc in next st, dc in each of next 8 sts, 3 dc in next st, dc in each of last 16 sts, turn. *(46 dc)*

Row 3: Ch 3, dc in each of next 15 sts, **dc dec** *(see Stitch Guide)* in next 3 sts, dc in each of next 8 sts, dc dec in next 3 sts, dc in each of last 16 sts, turn. *(42 dc)*

Row 4: Ch 3, dc in each of next 8 sts, dc dec in next 2 sts, (dc in each of next 9 sts, dc dec in next 2 sts] twice, dc in each of last 9 sts, turn. *(39 dc)*

Row 5: Ch 3, dc in each st across, turn.

Row 6: Ch 3, dc in each of next 11 sts, dc dec in next 2 sts, dc in each of next 11 sts, dc dec in next 2 sts, dc in each of last 12 sts, turn. *(37 dc)*

Row 7: Ch 3, dc in each of next 10 sts, dc dec in next 2 sts, dc in each of next 11 sts, dc dec in next 2 sts, dc in each of last 11 sts, turn. *(35 dc)*

Row 8: Ch 3, dc in each of next 9 sts, dc dec in next 2 sts, dc in each of next 11 sts, dc dec in next 2 sts, dc in each of last 10 sts, turn. *(33 dc)*

Row 9: Ch 3, dc in each of next 5 sts, 3 dc in next st, dc in each of next 6 sts, 3 dc in next st, dc in each of next 5 sts, [3 dc in next st, dc in each of next 6 sts] across, turn. *(41 dc)*

Row 10: Ch 3, dc in each of next 12 sts, [3 dc in next st, dc in each of next 13 sts] across, turn. *(45 dc)*

Rnd 11: Now working in rnds, ch 3, dc in each st around, **join** *(see Pattern Notes)* in 3rd ch of beg ch-3, **do not turn.**

Rnd 12: Ch 3, dc in each of next 9 sts, [2 dc in next st, dc in each of next 11 sts] twice, 2 dc in next st, dc in each of last 10 sts, join in 3rd ch of beg ch-3. *(48)*

Rnd 13: Ch 3, dc in each st around, join in 3rd ch of beg ch-3.

Rnd 14: Ch 3, dc in each of next 14 sts, dc dec in next 2 sts, dc in each of next 14 sts, dc dec in next 2 sts, dc in each of last 15 sts, join in 3rd ch of beg ch-3. *(46 dc)*

Rnd 15: Ch 3, dc in each st around, join in 3rd ch of beg ch-3.

Rnd 16: Ch 3, dc in each of next 13 sts, dc dec in next 2 sts, dc in each of next 14 sts, dc dec in next 2 sts, dc in each of last 14 sts, join in 3rd ch of beg ch-3. *(44 dc)*

Rnd 17: Ch 3, dc in each st around, join in 3rd ch of beg ch-3.

Rnd 18: Ch 3, dc in each of next 12 sts, dc dec in next 2 sts, dc in each of next 14 sts, dc dec in next 2 sts, dc in each of last 13 sts, join in 3rd ch of beg ch-3. *(42 dc)*

Rnd 19: Ch 3, dc in each st around, join in 3rd ch of beg ch-3.

Rnd 20: Ch 3, dc in each of next 11 sts, dc dec in next 2 sts, dc in each of next 14 sts, dc dec in next 2 sts, dc in each of last 12 sts, join in 3rd ch of beg ch-3. *(40 dc)*

Rnd 21: Ch 3, dc in each st around, join.

Rnd 22: Ch 3, dc in each of next 11 sts, [dc dec in next 2 sts, dc in each of next 12 sts] around, join in 3rd ch of beg ch-3. *(38 dc)*

Rnd 23: Ch 3, dc in each st around, join in 3rd ch of beg ch-3.

Rnd 24: Ch 3, dc in each of next 10 sts, dc dec in next 2 sts, dc in each of next 12 sts, dc dec in next 2 sts, dc in each of last 11 sts, join in 3rd ch of beg ch-3. *(36 dc)*

Rnds 25–27: Ch 3, dc in each st around, join in 3rd ch of beg ch-3.

Rnd 28: Ch 4 *(counts as first dc and ch-1),* [dc in next st, ch 1] around, join in 3rd ch of beg ch-4.

Rnd 29: Sl st in first ch sp, ch 3, dc in same ch sp, ch 2, [2 dc in next ch sp, ch 2] around, join in 3rd ch of beg ch-3.

Rnd 30: Sl st in next st, (sl st, ch 3, dc, ch 2, 2 dc) in next ch sp, (2 dc, ch 2, 2 dc) in each ch sp around, join in 3rd ch of beg ch-3.

Rnd 31: Sl st in next st, (sl st, ch 3, dc, ch 2, 2 dc) in next ch sp, ch 2, 2 dc in next ch sp, ch 2, *(2 dc, ch 2, 2 dc) in next ch sp, ch 2, 2 dc in next ch sp, ch 2, rep from * around, join in 3rd ch of beg ch-3.

Rnd 32: Sl st in next st, (sl st, ch 3, dc, ch 2, 2 dc) in next ch sp, 2 dc in next ch sp, ch 2, 2 dc in next ch sp, *(2 dc, ch 2, 2 dc) in next ch sp, 2 dc in next ch sp, ch 2, 2 dc in next ch sp, rep from * around, join in 3rd ch of beg ch-3.

Rnds 33 & 34: Sl st in next st, (sl st, ch 3, dc, ch 2, 2 dc) in next ch sp, (2 dc, ch 2, 2 dc) in each ch sp around, join in 3rd ch of beg ch-3. At end of last rnd, fasten off.

FINISHING

Sew 1 snap to ends of row 1 and 1 snap to end of row 9.

Glue or tack roses to Gown as shown in photo. ∎

Angora Sweater

SWEATER
SKILL LEVEL

EASY

FINISHED SIZE
Fits 11½-inch fashion doll

MATERIALS
- Fine (sport) weight yarn:
  1 oz/100 yds/28g white
- Size 0/2.50mm steel crochet hook
  or size needed to obtain gauge
- Sewing needle
- Matching sewing thread
- Small snaps: 4

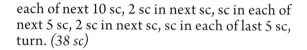

GAUGE
5 sc = 1 inch; 6 sc rows = 1 inch

PATTERN NOTES
After Sweater is completed, for fuzzy angora
look, brush Sweater with a stiff brush.

Join with slip stitch as indicated unless
otherwise stated.

INSTRUCTIONS
SWEATER
Row 1: Starting at neckline, ch 19, sc in 2nd ch
from hook, sc in each ch across, turn. *(18 sc)*

Row 2: Ch 1, sc in each of next 3 sc, 3 sc in next
sc, sc in next sc, 3 sc in next sc, sc in each of
next 6 sc, 3 sc in next sc, sc in next sc, 3 sc in
next sc, sc in each of last 3 sc, turn. *(26 sc)*

Row 3: Ch 1, sc in each of first 4 sc, 3 sc in
next sc, sc in each of next 3 sc, 3 sc in next sc,
sc in each of next 8 sc, 3 sc in next sc, sc in each
of next 3 sc, 3 sc in next sc, sc in each of last
4 sc, turn.

Row 4: Ch 1, sc in each of first 5 sc, 2 sc in next
sc, sc in each of next 5 sc, 2 sc in next sc, sc in

each of next 10 sc, 2 sc in next sc, sc in each of
next 5 sc, 2 sc in next sc, sc in each of last 5 sc,
turn. *(38 sc)*

Row 5: Ch 1, sc in each of first 6 sc, 3 sc in next
sc, sc in each of next 6 sc, 3 sc in next sc, sc in
each of next 10 sc, 3 sc in next sc, sc in each of
next 6 sc, 3 sc in next sc, sc in each of last 6 sc,
turn. *(46 sc)*

Row 6: Ch 1, sc in each of first 8 sc, ch 2, sk next
8 sc *(armhole)*, 2 sc in next sc, sc in each of next
12 sc, 2 sc in next sc, ch 2, sk next 8 sc *(armhole)*,
sc in each of last 8 sc, turn. *(2 ch-2 sps, 32 sc)*

Row 7: Ch 1, sc in each sc and in each ch across,
turn. *(36 sc)*

Row 8: Ch 1, sc in each of first 6 sc, **sc dec** *(see
Stitch Guide)* in next 2 sc, sc in each of next 2 sc,
sc dec in next 2 sc, sc in each of next 12 sc, sc
dec in next 2 sc, sc in each of next 2 sc, sc dec
in next 2 sc, sc in each of last 6 sc, turn. *(32 sc)*

Row 9: Ch 1, sc in each of first 5 sc, sc dec in
next 2 sc, sc in each of next 2 sc, sc dec in next
2 sc, sc in each of next 10 sc, sc dec in next 2 sc,
sc in each of next 2 sc, sc dec in next 2 sc, sc in
each of last 5 sc, turn. *(28 sc)*

Rows 10–17: Ch 1, sc in each sc across, turn.
At end of last row, fasten off.

SLEEVE
MAKE 2.
Rnd 1: Join with sc in first sc at top of armhole,
sc in each of next 8 sc, sc in end of row 6, sc dec
in next 2 sc, sc in end of row 6, **join** *(see Pattern
Notes)* in beg sc, **turn.** *(11 sc)*

Rnd 2: Ch 1, sc in each of first 2 sc, sc dec in
next 2 sc, sc in each sc around, join in beg sc,
turn. *(10 sc)*

Rnd 3: Ch 1, sc in each sc around, join in beg
sc, turn.

Rnd 4: Ch 1, sc in each of first 2 sc, sc dec in next 2 sc, sc in each sc around, join in beg sc. Fasten off. *(9 sc)*

FINISHING
Sew 4 snaps evenly sp down back opening.

Brush to fluff *(see Pattern Notes)*.

POODLE SKIRT
SKILL LEVEL

EASY

FINISHED SIZE
Fits 11½-inch fashion doll

MATERIALS
- Size 10 crochet cotton:
  1 ball pink
- Size 7/1.65mm steel crochet hook
  or size needed to obtain gauge
- Sewing needle
- Matching sewing thread
- Small snap
- 2 x 2½-inch piece white felt
- ⅛-inch ribbon: 6 inches

GAUGE
19 dc = 2 inches; 4 dc rnds = 1 inch

PATTERN NOTES
Chain-3 at beginning of row or round counts as first double crochet unless otherwise stated.

Join with slip stitch as indicated unless otherwise stated.

INSTRUCTIONS
SKIRT
Row 1: Beg at waist, ch 34, sc in 2nd ch from hook and in each ch across, turn. *(33 sc)*

Rows 2 & 3: Ch 1, sc in each st across, turn.

Row 4: Ch 3 *(see Pattern Notes)*, [dc in next sc, 2 dc in next sc] across, ending with 2 dc in last sc, turn. *(49 dc)*

Row 5: Ch 3, [dc in each of next 2 dc, 2 dc in next dc] across, turn. *(64 dc)*

Row 6: Ch 3, dc in each of next 2 dc, 2 dc in next dc, [dc in each of next 3 dc, 2 dc in next dc] across, turn. *(80 dc)*

Row 7: Ch 3, dc in each of next 3 dc, 2 dc in next dc, [dc in each of next 4 dc, 2 dc in next dc] across, turn. *(96 dc)*

Rnd 8: Now working in rnds, ch 3, dc in each of next 4 dc, 2 dc in next dc, [dc in each of next 5 dc, 2 dc in next dc] around, **join** *(see Pattern Notes)* in 3rd ch of beg ch-3, **turn.** *(112 dc)*

Rnd 9: Ch 3, dc in each of next 5 dc, 2 dc in next dc, [dc in each of next 6 dc, 2 dc in next dc] around, join in 3rd ch of beg ch-3, turn. *(128 dc)*

Rnd 10: Ch 3, dc in each of next 6 dc, 2 dc in next dc, [dc in each of next 7 dc, 2 dc in next dc] around, join in 3rd ch of beg ch-3, turn. *(144 dc)*

Rnd 11: Ch 3, dc in each of next 7 dc, 2 dc in next dc, [dc in each of next 8 dc, 2 dc in next dc] around, join in 3rd ch of beg ch-3, turn. *(160 dc)*

Rnd 12: Ch 3, dc in each of next 8 dc, 2 dc in next dc, [dc in each of next 9 dc, 2 dc in next dc] around, join in 3rd ch of beg ch-3, turn. *(176 dc)*

Rnd 13: Ch 3, dc in each of next 9 dc, 2 dc in next dc, [dc in each of next 10 dc, 2 dc in next dc] around, join in 3rd ch of beg ch-3, turn. *(192 dc)*

Rnd 14: Ch 3, dc in each of next 10 dc, 2 dc in next dc, [dc in each of next 11 dc, 2 dc in next dc] around, join in 3rd ch of beg ch-3, turn. *(208 dc)*

Rnd 15: Ch 3, dc in each of next 11 dc, 2 dc in next dc, [dc in each of next 12 dc, 2 dc in next dc] around, join in 3rd ch of beg ch-3, turn. *(224 dc)*

Rnd 16: Ch 3, dc in each of next 12 dc, 2 dc in next dc, [dc in each of next 13 dc, 2 dc in next dc] around, join in 3rd ch of beg ch-3, turn. *(240 dc)*

Rnd 17: Ch 3, dc in each of next 13 dc, 2 dc in next dc, [dc in each of next 14 dc, 2 dc in next dc] around, join in 3rd ch of beg ch-3, turn. *(256 dc)*

Rnd 18: Ch 3, dc in each of next 14 dc, 2 dc in next dc, [dc in each of next 15 dc, 2 dc in next dc] around, join in 3rd ch of beg ch-3, turn. Fasten off. *(272 dc)*

FINISHING

Sew snap to row 1 at back.

Cut poodle from felt, using full-size pattern piece *(see Fig. 1)*.

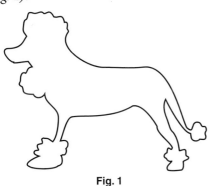

Fig. 1
Poodle Skirt
Full Size Pattern Piece

Glue or sew poodle to front of Skirt between rnds 11–16.

Tie ribbon in bow and tack to neck of poodle for collar as shown in photo.

Make ch long enough to reach from poodle collar to waist of Skirt. Tack ch in place.

BOBBY SOCKS
SKILL LEVEL
◖■ ◻ ◻
EASY

FINISHED SIZE
Fits 11½-inch fashion doll

MATERIALS
- Size 20 crochet cotton:
  25 yds light pink
- Size 9/1.25mm steel crochet

GAUGE
Work evenly and consistently.

PATTERN NOTE
Join with slip stitch as indicated unless otherwise stated.

INSTRUCTIONS
SOCK
MAKE 2.

Rnd 1: Beg at bottom of foot, ch 10, 3 sc in 2nd ch from hook, sc in each of next 7 chs, 3 sc in last ch, working on opposite side of ch, sc in each of next 7 chs, **join** *(see Pattern Note)* in beg sc. *(20 sc)*

Rnd 2: Ch 1, sc in each sc around, join in beg sc.

Rnd 3: Ch 1, **sc dec** *(see Stitch Guide)* in first 2 sc, sc dec in next 2 sc, sc in each sc around, join in beg sc. *(18 sc)*

Rnd 4: Ch 1, sc dec in first 2 sc, sc dec in next 2 sc, sc in each of next 12 sc, sc dec in last 2 sc, join in beg sc. *(15 sc)*

Rnd 5: Ch 1, sc dec in first 2 sc, sc in each of next 11 sc, sc dec in last 2 sc, join in beg sc. *(13 sc)*

RIBBING

Rnd 6: Ch 13, sc in 2nd ch from hook, sc in each of next 11 chs, [sl st in each of next 2 sc on rnd 5, ch 1, **turn**, working in **back lps** *(see Stitch Guide)*, sk sl sts just worked, sc in each of next 12 sc that was worked in ch, ch 1, **turn**, working in back lps, sc in each of next 12 sc] around, join in joining sl st of rnd 5. Fasten off.

Sew ends of Ribbing tog. ■

Rust & Peach Dress

DESIGN BY **JUANITA TURNER**

SKILL LEVEL

INTERMEDIATE

FINISHED SIZE
Fits 11½-inch fashion doll

MATERIALS
- Size 10 crochet cotton:
  85 yds dark coral
  30 yds light coral
- Size 7/1.65mm steel crochet hook
  or hook needed to obtain gauge
- Sewing needle
- Rust sewing thread
- Large gold ribbon roses: 2
- Straight pin
- Small snaps

GAUGE
9 sc = 1 inch; 11 sc rows = 1 inch

PATTERN NOTES
Chain-3 at beginning of row or round counts as
   first double crochet unless otherwise stated.

Join with slip stitch as indicated unless
   otherwise stated.

INSTRUCTIONS
DRESS
SKIRT
Row 1: Starting at waist, with dark coral, ch 29,
sc in 2nd ch from hook and in each ch across,
turn. *(28 sc)*

Row 2: Ch 1, sc in each st across, turn.

Row 3: Ch 1, sc in first st, 2 sc in next st, [sc
in next st, 2 sc in next st] across, turn. *(42 sc)*

Row 4: Ch 1, sc in each st across, turn.

Row 5: Ch 3 *(see Pattern Notes)*, dc in same st,
2 dc in each st across, turn. *(84 dc)*

Row 6: Ch 1, sc in each st across, turn.

Row 7: Ch 3, dc in each st across, turn.

Rows 8–10: [Rep rows 6 and 7 alternately]
twice, ending last rep with row 6.

Rnd 11: Now working in rnds, ch 3, dc in each
st around, **join** *(see Pattern Notes)* in 3rd ch of
beg ch-3, **turn.**

Rnd 12: Ch 1, sc in each st around, join in beg
sc, turn.

Rnds 13–19: [Rep rnds 11 and 12 alternately]
4 times, ending last rep with rnd 11.

Rnd 20: Working in **back lps** *(see Stitch Guide)*,
ch 1, sc in each st around, join in beg sc, turn.

Rnd 21: Ch 3, dc in each of next 2 sts, 2 dc
in next st, [dc in each of next 3 sts, 2 dc in
next st] around, join in 3rd ch of beg ch-3,
turn. *(105 dc)*

Rnd 22: Ch 1, sc in each st around, join in
beg sc. Fasten off.

UNDERSKIRT
Rnd 1: Working in rem lps of rnd 19 on Skirt,
join light coral in first st, ch 3, dc in each st
around, join 3rd ch of beg ch-3, **turn.** *(84 dc)*

Rnd 2: Ch 3, dc in each st around, join 3rd ch
of beg ch-3, turn.

Rnd 3: Ch 1, sc in each st around, join in beg
sc, turn.

Rnd 4: Working in back lps, ch 1, sc in first st, ch 3, [sc in next st, ch 3] around, join in beg sc, turn. Fasten off.

Rnd 5: Working in rem lps of rnd 3, join light coral with sc in first st, ch 3, [sc in next st, ch 3] around, join in beg sc. Fasten off.

BODICE

Row 1: Working in starting ch on opposite side of row 1 on Skirt, sk first 5 chs, join dark coral with sc in next ch, sc in each of next 15 chs leaving rem chs unworked, turn. *(16 sc)*

Row 2: Ch 1, sc in each st across, turn.

Row 3: Ch 1, 2 sc in first st, sc in each st across to last st, 2 sc in last st, turn. *(18 sc)*

Rows 4 & 5: Ch 1, sc in each st across, turn.

Rows 6–10: [Rep rows 3 and 4 alternately] 3 times, ending last rep with row 3. *(24 at end of last row)*

Row 11: Ch 1, sc in each of first 8 sts, 2 sc in each of next 8 sts, sc in each of last 8 sts, turn. *(32 sc)*

Rows 12–16: Ch 1, sc in each st across, turn.

Row 17: Ch 1, sc in each of first 6 sts, **sc dec** *(see Stitch Guide)* in next 2 sts, [sc in each of next 7 sts, sc dec in next 2 sts] twice, sc in each of last 6 sts, turn. *(29 sc)*

Row 18: Sl st in each of first 6 sts, sc dec in next 2 sts, sc in each of next 5 sts, sk next st, sc in next worked sc of row 14 *(to form dip at center front of Bodice)*, sk next st, sc in each of next 5 sts, sc dec in next 2 sts, sl st in each st across. Fasten off.

PLACKETS

Row 1: Working in rem starting ch on opposite side of row 1 on Skirt, join dark coral with sc in first ch, sc in each of next 5 chs, working in ends of rows on Bodice, evenly sp 12 sc across rows, turn. *(18 sc)*

Row 2: [Ch 3, sc in each of next 4 sts] twice, ch 3, sc in each of next 3 sts, ch 3, sl st in next st. Fasten off. *(4 ch-3 sps—used when lacing straps)*

Rep on opposite side of Skirt and Bodice.

FINISHING

Sew snap to back opening on Skirt.

STRAP

With light coral, ch 202, sc in 2nd ch from hook, sc in each of next 99 chs, 3 sc in next ch *(point)*, sc in each ch across. Fasten off.

Sew point of Strap over dip in center front of Bodice.

FINISHING

Place Dress on doll and lace ends of Strap back and forth through ch-3 sps. Tie in bow at bottom of Bodice.

Style hair and pin ribbon roses in place as desired. ■

Wine Dress

DESIGN BY JUANITA TURNER

SKILL LEVEL
INTERMEDIATE

FINISHED SIZE
Fits 11½-inch fashion doll

MATERIALS
- Size 10 rayon crochet thread:
  115 yds wine
- Size 10 crochet cotton:
  10 yds white
- No. 8 metallic braid:
  37 yds gold
- 4mm silk embroidery ribbon:
  18 inches green
- 7mm silk embroidery ribbon:
  18 inches white
- Size 7/1.65mm steel crochet hook
  or hook needed to obtain gauge
- Sewing needle
- Embroidery needle
- Matching sewing thread
- Gold ribbon roses:
  4 medium
  1 small
- Gold seed bead
- Straight pins: 5
- Small snaps: 4

GAUGE
9 sc = 1 inch; 11 sc rows = 1 inch

PATTERN NOTE
Join with slip stitch as indicated unless
  otherwise stated.

INSTRUCTIONS
DRESS
BODICE

Row 1: Starting at waist, with wine, ch 30, sc in 2nd ch from hook and in each ch across, turn. *(29 sc)*

Row 2: Ch 1, sc in each st across, turn.

Row 3: Ch 1, sc in each of first 10 sts, 2 sc in each of next 2 sts, sc in each of next 5 sts, 2 sc in each of next 2 sts, sc in each of last 10 sts, turn. *(33 sc)*

Row 4: Ch 1, sc in each of first 10 sts, 2 sc in each of next 2 sts, sc in each of next 9 sts, 2 sc in each of next 2 sts, sc in each of last 10 sts, turn. *(37 sc)*

Row 5: Ch 1, sc in each st across, turn.

Row 6: Ch 1, sc in each of first 10 sts, 2 sc in each of next 2 sts, sc in each of next 13 sts, 2 sc in each of next 2 sts, sc in each of last 10 sts, turn. *(41 sc)*

Rows 7 & 8: Ch 1, sc in each st across, turn.

Row 9: Ch 1, sc in each of first 12 sts, 2 sc in next st, sc in each of next 15 sts, 2 sc in next st, sc in each of last 12 sts, turn. *(43 sc)*

Rows 10 & 11: Ch 1, sc in each st across, turn.

Row 12: Ch 1, sc in each of first 12 sts, 2 sc in next st, sc in each of next 17 sts, 2 sc in next st, sc in each of last 12 sts, turn. *(45 sc)*

Row 13: Ch 1, sc in each st across, turn.

Row 14: Ch 1, sc in each of first 18 sts, 2 sc in each of next 9 sts, sc in each of last 18 sts, turn. *(54 sc)*

Rows 15–19: Ch 1, sc in each st across, turn.

Row 20: Ch 1, sc in each of first 8 sts, ch 16, sk next 9 sts *(armhole)*, sc in each of last 37 sts, turn. *(45 sc, 16 chs)*

Row 21: Ch 1, sc in each of first 26 sts, **sc dec** *(see Stitch Guide)* in next 2 sts, sc in each of next 8 sts, sk next st, sc in each of next 16 chs, sk next st, sl st in next st leaving rem sts unworked, turn. *(51 sc)*

Row 22: Ch 1, sc in each of first 16 sts, sl st in each of next 2 sts leaving rem sts unworked, turn. *(16 sc)*

Rows 23 & 24: Ch 1, sc in each st across, turn.

Row 25: Ch 1, sc in each of first 16 sts, sc in each of next 4 sts on row 22, turn. *(20 sc)*

Row 26: Ch 1, 2 sc in first st, sc in each of next 19 sts, sk next unworked st on row 22, sc in each of next 5 sts, sc in next worked st on row 14 *(to form dip at center front)*, sc in each st across. Fasten off.

SKIRT

Row 1: Working in starting ch on opposite side of row 1 on Bodice, join wine with sc in first ch, sc in each of next 6 chs, 2 sc in each of next 3 chs, sc in each of next 9 chs, 2 sc in each of next 3 chs, sc in each of last 7 chs, turn. *(35 sc)*

Row 2: Ch 1, sc in first st, [2 sc in next st, sc in next st] across, turn. *(52 sc)*

Rows 3–15: Ch 1, sc in each st across, turn.

Rnds 16–43: Now working in rnds, ch 1, sc in each st around, **join** *(see Pattern Note)* in beg sc, **turn**. At end of last rnd, fasten off.

Row 44: Now working in rows, sk first 21 sts, join with sc in next st, sc in each st across *(including sk sts at beg)* leaving last st unworked, turn. *(51 sc)*

Rows 45 & 46: Ch 1, sc in each st across, turn.

Row 47: Ch 1, sc in each of first 19 sts, sc dec in next 2 sts, sc in each st across, turn. *(50 sc)*

Row 48: Ch 1, sc in each of first 8 sts, sc dec in next 2 sts, sc in each of next 30 sts, sc dec in next 2 sts, sc in each of last 8 sts, turn. *(48 sc)*

Rows 49–84: Ch 1, sc in each st across, turn.

Rnd 85: Now working in rnds, ch 1, 2 sc in first st, sc in each of next 46 sts, 2 sc in last st, working in ends of rows, 2 sc in next row, evenly sp 38 sc across ends of rows, sl st in unworked st on row 43, working in ends of rows, evenly sp 38 sc across to last row, 2 sc in last row, join in beg sc. Fasten off.

Sew 4 snaps evenly sp down back opening of Dress.

CORSAGE

With silk ribbon and embroidery needle, embroider green leaves using **lazy daisy stitch** (*see Fig. 1*), **straight stitch** (*see Fig. 2*) and white **spiderweb rose** (*see Fig. 3*) as shown in photo.

Fig. 1
Lazy Daisy Stitch

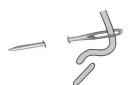

Fig. 2
Straight Stitch

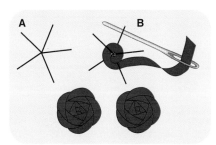

Stitch a 5-spoke web with thread or floss (A). Run the needle with ribbon up through center of the web; keeping the ribbon loose and allowing it to twist, weave the ribbon over one spoke and under the next spoke filling the spokes completely (B), then run the needle back to the back of the fabric at the edge of the rose.

Fig. 3
Spiderweb Rose

GLOVE
MAKE 2.

Rnd 1: Beg at top, with gold metallic braid, ch 14, sl st in first ch to form ring, ch 1, sc in each ch around, join in beg sc. (*14 sc*)

Rnds 2–12: Ch 1, sc in each st around, join in beg sc.

Rnd 13: Ch 1, sc in each of first 2 sts, sc dec in next 2 sts, sc in each of next 6 sts, sc dec in next 2 sts, sc in each of last 2 sts, join in beg sc. (*12 sc*)

Rnds 14 & 15: Ch 1, sc in each st around, join in beg sc.

Rnd 16: Ch 1, sc in each of first 2 sts, sc dec in next 2 sts, sc in each of next 4 sts, sc dec in next 2 sts, sc in each of last 2 sts, join in beg sc. (*10 sc*)

Rnds 17 & 18: Ch 1, sc in each st around, join in beg sc.

Rnd 19: Ch 1, sc in each of first 4 sts, 2 hdc in next st, ch 1, 2 hdc in next st, sc in each of last 4 sts, join in beg sc. (*12 sts*)

Rnd 20: Sl st in each of first 6 sts, 3 sc in next ch-1 sp, sl st in each of last 6 sts. Fasten off.

Place Glove on arm with 3 sc on rnd 20 at back of hand.

CLUTCH PURSE

Row 1: With gold metallic braid, ch 9, sc in 2nd ch from hook, sc in each ch across, turn. (*8 sc*)

Rows 2–13: Ch 1, sc in each st across, turn. At end of last row, fasten off.

Fold up last 5 rows, sl st ends of rows tog leaving 3 rows at top for flap.

BUTTON CLOSURE

String bead onto gold metallic braid and twist, forming a loop, tack to center front of Purse.

FINISHING

Style hair and glue or pin ribbon roses in place as desired. ■

Navy & Silver Dress

DESIGN BY JUANITA TURNER

SKILL LEVEL
INTERMEDIATE

FINISHED SIZE
Fits 11½-inch fashion doll

MATERIALS
- Size 10 rayon crochet thread:
  - 125 yds navy
  - 20 yds silver
- Size 7/1.65mm steel crochet hook or hook needed to obtain gauge
- Sewing needle
- Matching sewing thread
- Small silver ribbon roses: 3
- Straight pins: 3
- Small snaps: 2

GAUGE
9 sc = 1 inch; 11 sc rows = 1 inch

PATTERN NOTES
Chain-3 at beginning of row or round counts as first double crochet unless otherwise stated.

Join with slip stitch as indicated unless otherwise stated.

INSTRUCTIONS
DRESS
BODICE
Row 1: Starting at waist, with navy, ch 26, sc in 2nd ch from hook and in each ch across, turn. *(25 sc)*

Rows 2–6: Ch 1, sc in each st across, turn.

Row 7: Ch 1, **sc dec** *(see Stitch Guide)* in first 2 sts, sc in each st across to last 2 sts, sc dec in last 2 sts, turn. *(23 sc)*

Row 8: Ch 1, sc in each st across, turn.

Rows 9–11: Rep row 7. (*17 sc at end of last row*)

Row 12: Ch 1, sc in each st across, turn.

Row 13: Ch 3 (*see Pattern Notes*), dc in each of next 3 sts, 3 dc in each of next 3 sts, sk next st, sc in next st, sk next st, 3 dc in each of next 3 sts, dc in each of last 4 sts, turn. (*27 sts*)

Row 14: Ch 3, **dc dec** (*see Stitch Guide*) in next 2 sts, dc in each of next 9 sts, sk next st, sc in next st, sk next st, dc in each of next 9 sts, dc dec in next 2 sts, dc in last st, turn. (*23 sts*)

Row 15: Ch 3, dc dec in next 2 sts, dc in each of next 7 sts, sk next st, sc in next st, sk next st, dc in each of next 7 sts, dc dec in next 2 sts, dc in last st. Fasten off.

BODICE TRIM
Row 1: With silver, ch 62, sc in 2nd ch from hook, sc in each of next 29 chs, 3 sc in next ch (*center formed*), sc in each ch across, turn. (*63 sc*)

Row 2: Ch 1, sc in each of first 31 sts, 2 sc in next st, sc in each st across. Fasten off.

Leaving center 17 sts at front of Bodice unworked and 2 inches on center of Trim unworked, sew ends of Trim over ends of rows on each side of Bodice as shown in photo.

COLLAR
With navy, ch 22, sc in 2nd ch from hook, sc in each of next 9 chs, 3 sc in next ch (*center formed*), sc in each of last 10 chs. Fasten off.

Sew 1 snap to ends of Collar.

Slip Collar through opening of Bodice Trim and tack centers tog to secure.

SKIRT
Row 1: Working in starting ch on opposite side of row 1 on Bodice, join navy with sc in first ch, sc in each ch across, turn. (*25 sc*)

Row 2: Ch 1, 2 sc in each st across, turn. (*50 sc*)

Rows 3–9: Ch 1, sc in each st across, turn.

Row 10: Ch 1, sc in each of first 10 sts, sc dec in next 2 sts, sc in each of next 26 sts, sc dec in next 2 sts, sc in each of last 10 sts, turn. (*48 sc*)

Rows 11 & 12: Ch 1, sc in each st across, turn.

Rnds 13–26: Now working in rnds, ch 1, sc in each st around, **join** (*see Pattern Notes*) in beg sc, **turn**.

Rnd 27: Ch 1, sc in each of first 10 sts, sc dec in next 2 sts, sc in each of next 24 sts, sc dec in next 2 sts, sc in each of last 10 sts, join in beg sc, turn. (*46 sc*)

Rnds 28 & 29: Ch 1, sc in each st around, join, turn.

Rnd 30: Ch 1, sc in each of first 10 sts, sc dec in next 2 sts, sc in each of next 22 sts, sc dec in next 2 sts, sc in each of last 10 sts, join in beg sc, turn. (*44 sc*)

Rnds 31 & 32: Ch 1, sc in each st around, join in beg sc, turn.

Rows 33–35: Now working in rows, ch 1, sc in each st across, **do not join**, turn.

Row 36: Ch 1, sc in each of first 10 sts, sc dec in next 2 sts, sc in each of next 20 sts, sc dec in next 2 sts, sc in each of last 10 sts, turn. (*42 sc*)

Rows 37 & 38: Ch 1, sc in each st across, turn.

Row 39: Ch 1, sc in each of first 10 sts, sc dec in next 2 sts, sc in each of next 18 sts, sc dec in next 2 sts, sc in each of last 10 sts, turn. (*40 sc*)

Rows 40 & 41: Ch 1, sc in each st across, turn.

Row 42: Ch 1, sc in each of first 10 sts, sc dec in next 2 sts, sc in each of next 16 sts, sc dec in next 2 sts, sc in each of last 10 sts, turn. (*38 sc*)

Rows 43–69: Ch 1, sc in each st across, turn. At end of last row, fasten off.

FINISHING
Sew snap to back opening on Bodice.

Style hair and pin ribbon roses in place as desired. ∎

Blouse & Shorts

BLOUSE

SKILL LEVEL

EASY

FINISHED SIZE
Fits 11½-inch fashion doll

MATERIALS
- Size 10 crochet cotton:
  150 yds white
- Size 7/1.65mm steel crochet hook
  or size needed to obtain gauge
- Sewing needle
- Matching sewing thread
- 6mm buttons: 3

GAUGE
19 dc = 2 inches; 4 dc rows = 1 inch

PATTERN NOTE
Chain-3 at beginning of row counts as first
  double crochet unless otherwise stated.

SPECIAL STITCH
3-double crochet cluster (3-dc cl): Holding back
  last lp of each st on hook, 3 dc in each of next
  3 sts, yo, pull through all lps on hook.

INSTRUCTIONS
BLOUSE
Row 1: Beg at collar, ch 30, dc in 4th ch from
  hook *(first 3 chs count as first dc)* and in each
  ch across, turn. *(28 dc)*

Row 2: Ch 3 *(see Pattern Note)*, dc in each dc
  across, turn.

Row 3: Ch 1, sc in each of next 9 dc, sk next dc,
  sc in each of next 8 dc, sk next dc, sc in each of
  last 9 dc, turn. *(26 dc)*

Row 4: Ch 3, dc in each of next 4 sc, 3 dc in next
  sc, dc in each of next 2 sc, 3 dc in next sc, dc in
  each of next 8 sc, 3 dc in next sc, dc in each of
  next 2 sc, 3 dc in next sc, dc in each of last 5 sc,
  turn. *(34 dc)*

Row 5: Ch 3, dc in each of next 5 dc, 3 dc in next
  dc, dc in each of next 4 dc, 3 dc in next dc, dc in
  each of next 10 dc, 3 dc in next dc, dc in each of
  next 4 dc, 3 dc in next dc, dc in each of last 6 dc,
  turn. *(42 dc)*

Row 6: Ch 3, dc in each of next 6 dc, 3 dc in next
  dc, dc in each of next 6 dc, 3 dc in next dc, dc in
  each of next 12 dc, 3 dc in next dc, dc in each of
  next 6 dc, 3 dc in next dc, dc in each of last 7 dc,
  turn. *(50 dc)*

Row 7: Ch 3, dc in each of next 7 dc, 3 dc in next
  dc, dc in each of next 8 dc, 3 dc in next dc, dc in
  each of next 14 dc, 3 dc in next dc, dc in each of
  next 8 dc, 3 dc in next dc, dc in each of last 8 dc,
  turn. *(58 dc)*

Row 8: Ch 3, dc in each of next 8 dc, 2 dc in next
  dc, ch 3, sk next 10 dc *(armhole)*, 2 dc in next
  dc, dc in each of next 16 dc, 2 dc in next dc, ch
  3, sk next 10 dc *(armhole)*, 2 dc in next dc, dc in
  each of last 9 dc, turn. *(42 dc)*

Row 9: Ch 3, dc in each dc and in each ch across,
  turn. *(48 dc)*

Row 10: Ch 3, dc in each of next 3 dc, **3-dc cl** (*see Special Stitch*) in next 3 sts, dc in each of next 2 dc, **dc dec** (*see Stitch Guide*) in next 2 dc, dc in each of next 3 dc, dc dec in next 2 dc, dc in each of next 16 dc, dc dec in next 2 dc, dc in each of next 3 dc, dc dec in next 2 dc, dc in each of next 2 dc, 3-dc cl in next 3 dc, dc in each of last 4 dc, turn. (*40 dc*)

Row 11: Ch 3, dc in each of next 5 dc, dc dec in next 2 dc, dc in each of next 3 dc, dc dec in next 2 dc, dc in each of next 14 dc, dc dec in next 2 dc, dc in each of next 3 dc, dc dec in next 2 dc, dc in each of last 6 dc, turn. (*36 dc*)

Row 12: Ch 3, dc in each of next 4 dc, dc dec in next 2 dc, dc in each of next 3 dc, dc dec in next 2 dc, dc in each of next 12 dc, dc dec in next 2 dc, dc in each of next 3 dc, dc dec in next 2 dc, dc in each of last 5 dc, turn. (*32 dc*)

Row 13: Ch 3, dc in each of next 4 dc, 3 dc in next dc, dc in each of next 3 dc, 3 dc in next dc, dc in each of next 12 dc, 3 dc in next dc, dc in each of next 3 dc, 3 dc in next dc, dc in each of last 4 dc, turn. (*40 dc*)

Row 14: Ch 3, dc in each dc across. Fasten off.

FINISHING
Sew 3 buttons evenly sp to Front opening. Use sps between st opposite for button holes.

Fold and tack collar down.

SHORTS
SKILL LEVEL
■■□□
EASY

FINISHED SIZE
Fits 11½-inch fashion doll

MATERIALS
- Size 10 crochet cotton:
  100 yds red
- Size 7/1.65mm steel crochet hook
  or size needed to obtain gauge
- Sewing needle
- Matching sewing thread
- Small snap

GAUGE
19 dc = 2 inches; 4 dc rows = 1 inch

PATTERN NOTES
Chain-3 at beginning of row or round counts as first double crochet unless otherwise stated.

Join with slip stitch as indicated unless otherwise stated.

INSTRUCTIONS
Row 1: Beg at waist, ch 34, sc in 2nd ch from hook and in each ch across, turn. *(33 sc)*

Rows 2 & 3: Ch 1, sc in each sc across, turn.

Row 4: Ch 3 *(see Pattern Note)*, dc in each of next 7 sc, 3 dc in next sc, dc in each of next 2 sc, 3 dc in next sc, dc in each of next 12 sc, 3 dc in next sc, dc in each of next 2 sc, 3 dc in next sc, dc in each of last 5 sc, turn. *(41 dc)*

Row 5: Ch 3, [dc in each of next 5 dc, 3 dc in next dc] twice, dc in each of next 12 dc, 3 dc in next dc, dc in each of next 6 dc, 3 dc in next dc, dc in each of last 8 dc, turn. *(49 dc)*

Row 6: Ch 3, dc in each of next 7 dc, 2 dc in next dc, dc in each of next 10 dc, 2 dc in next dc, dc in each of next 12 dc, 2 dc in next dc, dc in each of next 10 dc, 2 dc in next dc, dc in each of last 5 dc, turn. *(53 dc)*

Row 7: Ch 3, dc in each dc across, turn.

Rnd 8: Now working in rnds, ch 3, dc in each dc around, **join** *(see Pattern Notes)* in 3rd ch of beg ch-3, turn.

Rnd 9: Joining in top of 2nd dc after beg ch-3 creates an overlap for a neat waist closing, ch 3, working through both thicknesses by sliding hook in top of next dc and also the dc behind it, work dc, work next dc in top of beg ch-3 and the dc behind it, dc in each dc around, join in 3rd ch of beg ch-3. *(50 dc)*

FIRST LEG
Rnd 10: Sl st in next dc, ch 2, sk next 24 dc, join in next dc, turn.

Rnd 11: Ch 3, dc in each of next 2 chs, dc in each of next 24 dc, join in 3rd ch of beg ch-3, turn. *(27 dc)*

Rnds 12 & 13: Ch 3, dc in each dc around, join in 3rd ch of beg ch-3, turn. At end of last rnd, fasten off.

2ND LEG
Rnd 11: Join in dc to right of ch-2, ch 3, dc in each of next 2 chs, dc in each of next 24 dc, join in 3rd ch of beg ch-3. *(27 dc)*

Rnds 12 & 13: Ch 3, dc in each dc around, join in 3rd ch of beg ch-3, turn. At end of last rnd, fasten off.

FINISHING
Sew snap to rnd 1 in back. Fold rnd 13 of First and 2nd Legs upward for cuff and tack in place. ■

Bedroom Jazz

RUG

SKILL LEVEL

EASY

FINISHED SIZE

3¼ x 12¾ inches

MATERIALS

- Medium (worsted) weight yarn:
  2 oz/100yds/57g red
  1 oz/50 yds/28g black
- Size F/5/3.75mm crochet hook
  or size needed to obtain gauge

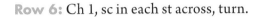

GAUGE

4 sc = 1 inch; 9 sc rows = 2 inches

SPECIAL STITCH

Join with half double crochet (join with hdc):
Place slip knot on hook, yo, insert hook in place indicated, yo, pull lp through, yo, pull through all lps on hook.

INSTRUCTIONS

RUG

Row 1: With red, ch 32, 2 sc in 2nd ch from hook, [sc in each of next 5 chs, 2 sc in next ch] 5 times, turn. *(37 sc)*

Row 2: Ch 1, sc in each st across, turn.

Row 3: Ch 1, 2 sc in first st, sc in each of next 7 sts, 2 sc in next st, [sc in each of next 6 sts, 2 sc in next st] 4 times, turn. *(43 sc)*

Row 4: Ch 1, sc in each st across, turn.

Row 5: Ch 1, 2 sc in first st, sc in each of next 10 sts, 2 sc in next st, [sc in each of next 9 sts, 2 sc in next st] twice, sc in each of next 10 sts, 2 sc in last st, turn. *(48 sc)*

Row 6: Ch 1, sc in each st across, turn.

Row 7: Ch 1, 2 sc in first st, sc in each of next 11 sts, 2 sc in next st, [sc in each of next 10 sts, 2 sc in next st] twice, sc in each of next 12 sts, 2 sc in last st, turn. *(53 sc)*

Row 8: Ch 1, sc in each st across, turn.

Row 9: Ch 1, **sc dec** *(see Stitch Guide)* in first 2 sts, sc in each of next 12 sts, 2 sc in next st, [sc in each of next 11 sts, 2 sc in next st] twice, sc in each of next 12 sts, sc dec in last 2 sts, turn. *(54 sc)*

Row 10: Ch 1, sc dec in first 2 sts, sc in each st across to last 2 sts, sc dec in last 2 sts, turn. *(52 sc)*

Row 11: Ch 1, sc dec in first 2 sts, sc in each of next 11 sts, 2 sc in next st, [sc in each of next 12 sts, 2 sc in next st] twice, sc in each of next 10 sts, sc dec in last 2 sts, turn. (53 sc)

Row 12: Ch 1, sc dec in first 2 sts, sc in each st across to last 2 sts. sc dec in last 2 sts, turn. (51 sc)

Row 13: Ch 1, sc dec in first 2 sts, sc in each of next 10 sts, 2 sc in next st, [sc in each of next 12 sts, 2 sc in next st] twice, sc in each of next 10, sc dec in last 2 sts, turn. (52 sc)

Row 14: Ch 1, sc dec in first 2 sts, sc in each st across to last 2 sts, sc dec in last 2 sts, do not turn.

FIRST SIDE
Working in ends of rows, sl st in end of each row down side. Fasten off.

2ND SIDE
Join red with sl st in end of row 1 on other side of Rug, sl st in end of each row up side. Fasten off.

TRIM
Working in **back loops** (see Stitch Guide) of sl sts on side edges and in row 14 on outer edge of Rug, join black with hdc (see Special Stitch) in first st on 2nd Side, placing 2 sts in 1 where necessary to make Rug lie flat, evenly sp hdc across to end of First Side. Fasten off.

COVERLET
SKILL LEVEL

INTERMEDIATE

FINISHED SIZE
9 inches in diameter

MATERIALS
- Medium (worsted) weight yarn:
  3 oz/150yds/85g red
  1 oz/50 yds/28g gold
- Size F/5/3.75mm crochet hook or size needed to obtain gauge

GAUGE
4 dc = 1 inch; 9 dc rnds = 2 inches

PATTERN NOTES
Chain-3 at beginning of row or round counts as first double crochet unless otherwise stated.

Join with slip stitch as indicated unless otherwise stated.

SPECIAL STITCHES
Top Left Bar of double crochet (top left bar of dc): Insert hook under the vertical bar just below the 2 top lps on left-hand side of st (see Fig. 1).

Fig. 1
Top Left Bar of Double Crochet

2 Left Loops at base of double crochet (2 left lps at base of dc): Insert hook between the 2 front vertical lps at the base of the st, placing the back vertical lp on same side of hook as left-hand lp (see Fig. 2).

Fig. 2
2 Left Loops at Base of Double Crochet

INSTRUCTIONS
COVERLET
Rnd 1: With red, ch 5, sl st in first ch to form ring, **ch 3** (see Pattern Notes), 13 dc in ring, **join** (see Pattern Notes) in 3rd ch of beg ch 3. (14 dc)

Note: All rnds are worked in the **top left bar of dc** (see Special Stitches).

Rnd 2: Ch 1, sc in next dc, ch 2, dc in side of sc just made *dc in next st, dc in **2 left lps at base of dc** just made (see Special Stitches), rep from * around, dc in 2nd ch of ch 3 on last rnd, dc in 2 left lps at base of dc just made, join in 2nd ch of beg ch 2. (28 dc)

Rnd 3: Sc in next dc, ch 2, [dc in next st, dc in 2 left lps at base of dc just made, dc in next st] around, dc in first ch of ch 2 on last rnd, dc in 2 left lps at base of dc just made, join in 2nd ch of beg ch-2. (42 dc)

Rnd 4: Sc in next dc, ch 2, dc in next st, [dc in next st, dc in 2 left lps at base of dc just made, dc in each of next 2 sts] around, dc in first ch of ch-2 on last rnd, dc in 2 left lps at base of dc just made, join in 2nd ch of beg ch-2. (*56 dc*)

Rnd 5: Sc in next dc, ch 2, dc in each of next 2 sts, [dc in next st, dc in 2 left lps at base of dc just made, dc in each of next 3 sts] around, dc in first ch of ch-2 on last rnd, dc in 2 left lps at base of dc just made, join in 2nd ch of beg ch-2. (*70 dc*)

Rnd 6: Sc in next dc, ch 2, dc in each of next 3 sts, [dc in next st, dc in 2 left lps at base of dc just made, dc in each of next 4 sts] around, dc in first ch of ch-2 on last rnd, dc in 2 left lps at base of dc just made, join in 2nd ch of beg ch-2. (*84 dc*)

Rnd 7: Sc in next dc, ch 2, dc in each of next 4 sts, [dc in next st, dc in 2 left lps at base of dc just made, dc in each of next 5 sts] around, dc in first ch of ch-2 on last rnd, dc in 2 left lps at base of dc just made, join in 2nd ch of beg ch-2. (*98 dc*)

Rnd 8: Sc in next dc, ch 2, dc in each of next 5 sts, [dc in next st, dc in 2 left lps at base of dc just made, dc in each of next 6 sts] around, dc in first ch of ch-2 on last rnd, dc in 2 left lps at base of dc just made, join in 2nd ch of beg ch-2. (*112 dc*)

Rnd 9: Sc in next dc, ch 2, dc in each of next 6 sts, [dc in next st, dc in 2 left lps at base of dc just made, dc in each of next 7 sts] around, dc in first ch of ch-2 on last rnd, dc in 2 left lps at base of dc just made, join in 2nd ch of beg ch-2. Fasten off. (*126 dc*)

EDGING
Join gold in any st of last rnd, ch 1, working from left to right, **reverse sc** (*see Fig. 3*) in each st around, join in beg reverse sc. Fasten off.

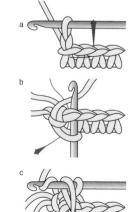

Fig. 3
Reverse Single Crochet

BED
SKILL LEVEL
INTERMEDIATE

FINISHED SIZE
11 inches across without Side Tables

MATERIALS
- Medium (worsted) weight yarn: 6 oz/300yds/170g black
- Size F/5/3.75mm crochet hook or size needed to obtain gauge
- Tapestry needle
- 9-inch circle of 1-inch thick foam
- Fiberfill
- Craft glue

GAUGE
4 sc = 1 inch; 9 sc rnds = 2 inches

PATTERN NOTES
Chain-3 at beginning of row or round counts as first double crochet unless otherwise stated.

Join with slip stitch as indicated unless otherwise stated.

SPECIAL STITCH
Front post double crochet decrease (fpdc dec): Holding back last lp of each st on hook, fpdc around each of next 2 sts, yo, pull through all lps on hook.

INSTRUCTIONS
BED
FRAME
Rnd 1: Ch 98, sl st in first ch to form ring, **ch 3** (*see Pattern Notes*), dc in each of next 5 chs, 2 dc in next ch, [dc in each of next 6 chs, 2 dc in next ch] around, **join** (*see Pattern Notes*) in 3rd ch of beg ch-3, **turn.** (*112 dc—Bottom Rim completed*)

Rnd 2: Working this rnd in **back lps** (*see Stitch Guide*), ch 1, sc in each of first 6 sts, 2 sc in next st, [sc in each of next 6 sts, 2 sc in next st] around, join in beg sc, turn. (*128 sc*)

Rnds 3–9: Working in both lps, ch 1, sc in each st around, join in beg sc, turn.

Rnd 10: Ch 1, **sc dec** *(see Stitch Guide)* in first 2 sts, sc in each of next 6 sts, [sc dec in next 2 sts, sc in each of next 6 sts] around, join in beg sc, turn. *(112 sc)*

Rnd 11: Working in sts of last rnd and rem lps of rnd 1 at same time *(this "sews" the edges tog as you work)*, sc in each st around, stuffing lightly with fiberfill as you go, join in beg sc, turn.

Rnd 12: Working this rnd in **front lps** *(see Stitch Guide)* only, ch 3, dc in each of next 5 sts, 2 dc in next st, [dc in each of next 6 sts, 2 dc in next st] around, join in 3rd ch of beg ch-3, turn. *(128 dc)*

Rnd 13: Working this rnd in back lps only, ch 1, sc in each st around, join in beg sc, turn.

Rem front lps of rnd 12 are on inside of Base and will be used later.

Rnds 14–20: Rep rnds 3–9.

Rnd 21: Ch 1, sc dec in first 2 sts, sc in each of next 6 sts, [sc dec in next 2 sts, sc in each of next 6 sts] around, join in beg sc, turn. *(112 sc)*

Rnd 22: Working in sts of last rnd and rem front lps of rnd 12 at the same time, ch 3, dc in each st around, stuffing lightly with fiberfill as you go, join in 3rd ch of beg ch-3, **do not turn.**

TOP RIM

Rnd 23: Ch 1, **fpsc** *(see Stitch Guide)* around ch-3 on rnd below, ch 2, **fpdc** *(see Stitch Guide)* around each of next 5 sts, **fpdc dec** *(see Special Stitch)*, [fpdc around each of next 6 sts, fpdc dec] around, join in 2nd ch of beg ch-2. Fasten off.

TOP BOLSTER

Rnd 1: Ch 15, sl st in first ch to form ring, ch 1, sc in each ch around, join in beg sc. *(15 sc)*

Rnd 2: Ch 1, sc in each of first 15 sts, **do not join rnds.**

Rnd 3: Sk ch-1, sc in each of next 15 sts.

Rnd 4: Sc in each of next 15 sts.

Next rnds: Rep rnd 4 until piece measures about 14 inches in length. At end of last rnd, join in beg sc. Fasten off.

Stuff with fiberfill. Flatten 1 end of crocheted tube and sew edges tog.

Rep at other end of crocheted tube.

BOTTOM BOLSTER

Rnd 1: Ch 2, 5 sc in 2nd ch from hook, **do not join rnds.** *(5 sc)*

Rnd 2: 2 sc in each st around. *(10 sc)*

Rnd 3: [Sc in next st, 2 sc in next st] around. *(115 sc)*

Rnd 4: Sc in each st around.

Next rnds: Rep rnd 4 until piece measures 10 inches in length. Stuff with fiberfill.

Next rnd: [Sc dec in next 2 sts, sc in next st] around. *(10 sc)*

Last rnd: [Sc dec in next 2 sts] around. Leaving long end, fasten off.

Weave long end through sts of last rnd. Pull to close opening. Secure end.

FINISHING

1. Insert foam circle inside Bed Frame so Bottom and Top Rims fit over edges of circle.

2. Position Bottom Bolster on top edge of Bed *(see Fig. 4)* and glue in place.

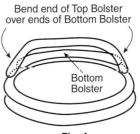

Bend end of Top Bolster over ends of Bottom Bolster

Bottom Bolster

Fig. 4
Bed Assembly Diagram

3. Center Top Bolster over Bottom Bolster. The ends will extend past ends of Bottom Bolster; glue in place.

4. Bend extended ends of Top Bolster over ends of Bottom Bolster and glue to top edge of Bed.

5. Place Coverlet on top Bed, covering Top Rim of Bed.

SIDE TABLE
SKILL LEVEL

INTERMEDIATE

FINISHED SIZE
4½ inches across

MATERIALS
- Medium (worsted) weight yarn: 2 oz/100 yds/57g black
- Size F/5/3.75mm crochet hook or size needed to obtain gauge
- Tapestry needle
- 3-inch cardboard circle: 2
- 2¾-inch circle of 1-inch thick foam: 2
- Foil
- Craft glue

GAUGE
4 sc = 1 inch; 9 sc rnds = 2 inches

INSTRUCTIONS
TABLE
MAKE 2.
Rnd 1: Ch 2, 6 sc in 2nd ch from hook, **do not join or turn**. (*6 sc*)

Row 2: Now working in rows, 2 sc in each st across, turn. (*12 sc*)

Row 3: Ch 1, sc in first st, 2 sc in next st, [sc in next st, 2 sc in next st] 3 times, sc in next st, leaving rem sts unworked, turn. (*13 sc*)

Row 4: Ch 1, sc in each of first 2 sts, 2 sc in next st, [sc in each of next 2 sts, 2 sc in next st] 3 times, sc in last st, turn. (*17 sc*)

Row 5: Ch 1, sc in each of first 3 sts, 2 sc in next st, [sc in each of next 3 sts, 2 sc in next st] 3 times, sc in last st, turn. (*21 sc*)

Row 6: Ch 1, sc in each of first 4 sts, 2 sc in next st, [sc in each of next 4 sts, 2 sc in next st] 3 times, sc in last st, turn. (*25 sc*)

Row 7: Working this row in **back lps** (*see Stitch Guide*), ch 1, sc in each st across, turn.

Row 8: Working this row in back lps only, ch 1, sc in first st, 2 sc in next st, [sc in next st, 2 sc in next st] 11 times, sc in last st, turn. (*37 sc*)

Rows 9–14: Working in both lps, sc in each st across, turn.

Row 15: Ch 1, sc in first st, **sc dec** (*see Stitch Guide*) in next 2 sts, [sc in next st, sc dec in next 2 sts] 11 times, sc in last st, turn. (*25 sc*)

Row 16: Working in sts of last row and rem lps of row 7 at same time, ch 1, sc in each st across, stuffing as you go, turn.

The piece can be stuffed lightly after the row is finished by pushing fiberfill into each end with a pencil.

Row 17: Ch 1, sc in each st across, turn.

Rows 18–25: Rep rows 8–15.

Row 26: Working in sts of last row and rem front loops of row 17 at same time, ch 1, sc in each st across, stuffing as you go. Fasten off.

FINISHING
1. Position ends of each Table on each side of Bed Frame as shown in photo and pin in place. Securely tack ends in place.

2. Apply craft glue to 1 side of 1 foam circle and insert inside center opening of 1 Table, pressing glued side to bottom.

3. Cover 3-inch cardboard circles with foil for mirrors.

4. Apply craft glue to back of a mirror and insert into center opening over foam with edges of mirror under row 26 of Table and between rolls on Bed Frame, press glued side on foam.

5. Rep for other Table.

DRESSING TABLE & STOOL

SKILL LEVEL

INTERMEDIATE

FINISHED SIZE
Dressing Table is 3 inches tall,
excluding mirrors

MATERIALS
- Medium (worsted) weight yarn:
  3 oz/150yds/85g red
  2 oz/100 yds/57g black
- Size F/5/3.75mm and H/8/5mm
  crochet hooks or size needed
  to obtain gauge
- Tapestry needle
- Cardboard:
  3-inch circle: 1
  1½-inch circles: 2
  5 x 8 inch piece: 1
- Foil
- 20-inch piece of florist wire
- Craft glue
- Stitch marker

GAUGE
Size F hook: 4 sc = 1 inch; 9 sc rnds = 2 inches

Size H hook: 4 sc = 1 inch; 4 sc back lp rows = 1 inch

PATTERN NOTES
Do not join or turn rounds unless
otherwise stated.

Mark first stitch of each round.

INSTRUCTIONS
DRESSING TABLE
BASE
CENTER PIECE
MAKE 2.
Row 1: With size H hook and red, ch 11,
sc in 2nd ch from hook, sc in each ch
across, turn. *(10 sc)*

Rows 2–20: Working in **back lps** *(see Stitch Guide)* *only*, ch 1, sc in each st across, turn.
At end of last row, fasten off.

FIRST END
Row 1: Hold both Center Pieces tog, matching
last row on each piece tog, working through
both thicknesses, with size H hook , join red
with sc in first st, sc in each st across, turn.

Rows 2–20: Working in back lps, ch 1, sc in each
st across, turn. At end of last row, fasten off.

2ND END
Row 1: Hold other end of both Center Pieces
tog, working through both thicknesses, with
size H hook, join red with sc in first st, sc in
each st across, turn.

Rows 2–20: Working in back lps only, ch 1,
sc in each st across, turn. At end of last row,
fasten off.

Glue layers in place as you work and roll up
each End to form columns at each end of
Base Center.

TOP PIECE
MAKE 1 BLACK & 1 RED.
Rnd 1: With size F hook, ch 13, 2 sc in 2nd ch
from hook sc in each of next 10 chs, 3 sc in last
ch, working on opposite side of ch, sc in each
of next 11 chs, **do not join rnds** *(see Pattern
Notes)*. *(26 sc)*

Rnd 2: 2 sc in each of next 2 sts, [sc in each of next 3 sts, 2 sc in next st] twice, sc in each of next 2 sts, 2 sc in each of next 3 sts, [sc in each of next 2 sts, **sc dec** (see Stitch Guide) in next 2 sts] twice, sc in each of next 3 sts. (31 sc)

Rnd 3: 2 sc in each of next 4 sts, [sc in each of next 4 sts, 2 sc in next st] twice, sc in each of next 4 sts, 2 sc in each of next 5 sts, [sc dec in next 2 sts, sc in each of next 2 sts] twice. (40 sc)

Rnd 4: Sk next st, [2 sc in next st, sc in next st] 4 times, sc in each of next 15 sts, [2 sc in next st, sc in next st] 4 times, sc in each of next 5 sts, sk next st, sc in each of next 5 sts, you will be working over first sts of rnd, beg of rnds will shift. (46 sc)

Rnd 5: [2 sc in next st, sc in each of next 2 sts] 4 times, sc in each of next 4 sts, 2 sc in next st, sc in each of next 8 sts, [2 sc in next st, sc in each of next 2 sts] 4 times, sc in each of next 10 sts. (55 sc)

Rnd 6: [2 sc in next st, sc in each of next 3 sts] 4 times, 2 sc in next st, sc in each of next 8 sts, 2 sc in next st, [sc in each of next 3 sts, 2 sc in next st] 4 times, sc in each of next 15 sts. (65 sc)

Rnd 7: [2 sc in next st, sc in each of next 4 sts] 4 times, 2 sc in next st, sc in each of next 15 sts, 2 sc in next st, [sc in each of next 4 sts, 2 sc in next st] 3 times, sc in each of next 2 sts, sl st in next st. Fasten off.

FINISHING

Using 1 crocheted piece as a pattern, trace outline of Top Piece onto cardboard and cut about ⅛ inch smaller than crochet piece.

With black Piece facing you, hold both Top Pieces with WS tog, working through both thicknesses, with size F hook, join red with sl st in any st, sl st in each st around, inserting cardboard piece inside before closing, join with sl st in beg sl st. Fasten off.

Curve Base Center slightly to match curved back edge of Top (see Fig. 5).

Glue shaped Base to red side of assembled Top.

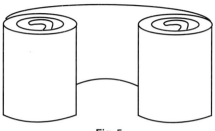

Fig. 5
Dressing Table Base Center
Diagram

STOOL BASE LAYER
MAKE 1 RED & 1 BLACK.

Rnd 1: With size F hook, ch 18, sl st in first ch to form ring, ch 1, sc in first ch, 2 sc in next ch, [sc in next ch, 2 sc in next ch] around, do not join rnds. (27 sc)

Rnds 2–7: Sc in each st around.

Rnd 8: [Sc in next st, sc dec in next 2 sts] around.

Rnd 9: Fold last rnd of crochet tube down to match first rnd and lightly stuff inside of folded tube, matching sts and working through both thicknesses, sc in each st around, join with sl st in beg sc. Fasten off.

FINISHING
Stack Base Layers and glue or tack tog.

STOOL CUSHION SIDE
MAKE 2.

Rnd 1: With size F hook and black, ch 2, 6 sc in 2nd ch from hook, **do not join rnds.** (6 sc)

Rnd 2: 2 sc in each st around.

Rnd 3: [Sc in next st, 2 sc in next st] around.

Rnd 4: [Sc in each of next 2 sts, 2 sc in next st] around, sl st in first sc. Fasten off.

Hold both Cushion Side pieces with WS tog, working through both thicknesses, join black with sl st in any st on rnd 4, sl st in each st around, join with sl st in beg sc. Fasten off.

Glue or tack Cushion to top of red Layer of assembled Base.

OPTIONAL MIRROR

1. Cover cardboard circles with foil.

2. Cut 1 piece of wire 8 inches long and cut 2 pieces each 6-inches long.

3. Shape wire (see Fig. 6).

Fig. 6
Mirror Stand
Wire Diagram

4. Glue the 8-inch piece to large mirror and each 6-inch piece to back of each small mirror.

5. Attach to Table as shown in photo.

THROW PILLOWS

SKILL LEVEL

INTERMEDIATE

FINISHED SIZES

Range in size from 2½ inches to 5 inches

MATERIALS

- Medium (worsted) weight yarn: 1 oz/50 yds/28g each purple, lavender, gold, orange, red, blue and green
- Size F/5/3.75mm crochet hook or size needed to obtain gauge
- Fiberfill

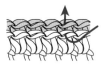
MEDIUM

GAUGE

4 sc = 1 inch; 9 sc rnds = 2 inches

PATTERN NOTES

Do not join or turn rounds unless otherwise stated.

Mark first stitch of each round.

Chain-3 at beginning of row or round counts as first double crochet unless otherwise stated.

Join with slip stitch as indicated unless otherwise stated.

INSTRUCTIONS
PURPLE PILLOW
SIDE
MAKE 2.

Row 1: With purple, loosely ch 14, sc in 2nd ch from hook and in each ch across, turn. (13 sc)

Rows 2–12: Ch 1, sc in each st across, turn.

Rnd 13: Now working in rnds, ch 1, sc in each st across, working in ends of rows and loosely enough to keep edge from curling, sl st in end of each row down side, working in starting ch on opposite side of row 1, sl st in each ch across, working in ends of rows and loosely enough to keep edge from curling, sl st in end of each row up side, **join** (see Pattern Notes) in beg sc. Fasten off.

RUFFLE

Matching sts and end of rows, hold both Pillow Side pieces with WS tog, working in **inside lps** (see Fig. 7) all the way around, this will "sew" the Pillow Sides tog as you add the Ruffle, join purple with sl st in first set of inside lps after corner, **ch 3** (see Pattern Notes), 3 dc in each st around outer edge, stuffing with fiberfill before closing, join with sl st in 3rd ch of beg ch-3. Fasten off.

Fig. 7
Inside Loops

ORANGE & HOT RED
SIDE
MAKE 2.

Row 1: With orange, loosely ch 10, sc in 2nd ch from hook and in each ch across, turn. (9 sc)

Rows 2–8: Ch 1, sc in each st across, turn.

Rnd 9: Now working in rnds, ch 1, sc in each st across, working in ends of rows and loosely enough to keep edge from curling, sl st in end of each row down side, working in starting ch on opposite side of row 1, sl st in each ch across, working in ends of rows and loosely enough to keep edge from curling, sl st in end of each row up side, **join** (see Pattern Notes) in beg sc. Fasten off.

BORDER

Matching sts and ends of rows, hold both Pillow Side pieces with WS tog, join hot red with sc in first set of **inside lps** (see Fig. 7) on Edge, sc in each set of inside lps around outer edge with (sc, ch 1, sc) at each corner, stuffing Pillow with fiberfill before you finish Border, join with sl st in beg sc. Fasten off.

GOLD & ORANGE PILLOW
SIDE
MAKE 2.

Row 1: With gold, loosely ch 11, sc in 2nd ch from hook and in each ch across, turn. (10 sc)

Rows 2–11: Ch 1, sc in each st across, turn.

Rnd 12: Now working in rnds, ch 1, sc in each st across, working in ends of rows and loosely enough to keep edge from curling, sl st in end of each row down side, working in starting ch on opposite side of row 1, sl st in each ch across, working in ends of rows and loosely enough to keep edge from curling, sl st in end of each row up side, **join** (see Pattern Notes) in beg sc. Fasten off.

BORDER

Matching sts and ends of rows, hold both Pillow Side pieces with WS tog, join orange with sl st in first set of **inside lps** (see Fig. 7) on Edge, ch 1, working from left to right, **reverse sc** (see Fig. 8) in each set of inside lps around outer edge, stuffing Pillow before you finish Border, join with sl st in first reverse sc. Fasten off.

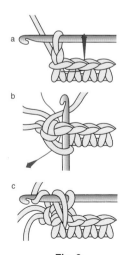

Fig. 8
Reverse Single Crochet

LAVENDER & ORANGE BOLSTER PILLOW

Rnd 1: With lavender, ch 2, 5 sc in 2nd ch from hook, **do not join rnds** (see Pattern Notes). (5 sc)

Rnd 2: 2 sc in each st around, **changing colors** (see Stitch Guide) to orange in last st. Fasten off lavender. (10 sc)

Rnd 3: Working in **back lps** (see Stitch Guide), sc in each st around.

Rnds 4–9: Working in both lps, sc in each st around.

Rnd 10: Sc in each st around, changing to lavender in last st. Fasten off orange.

Rnd 11: Working in back lps, sc in each st around. Stuff with fiberfill.

Rnd 12: Working in both loops, [**sc dec** (see Stitch Guide) in next 2 sts] around. (5 sc)

Rnd 13: Sl st in every other st to close opening. Fasten off.

BLUE & PURPLE PILLOW

Rnd 1: With blue, ch 4, sl st in first ch to form ring, **ch 3** (see Pattern Notes), 11 dc in ring, **join** (see Pattern Notes) in 3rd ch of beg ch 3. (12 dc)

Rnd 2: Ch 3, **fpdc** (see Stitch Guide) around ch-3 below, [dc in next dc, fpdc around same dc] around, join in 3rd ch of beg ch-3. Fasten off.

BORDER

Hold Pillow Side pieces with WS tog, join purple with sc in first set of **inside lps** (see Fig. 7) on Edge, sc in each set of inside lps around outer edge, stuffing Pillow before you finish Border, join in beg sc. Fasten off.

GREEN & BLUE PILLOW
SIDE
MAKE 2.

Row 1: With green, ch 9, sc in 2nd ch from hook, sc in each ch across, turn. (8 sc)

Row 2: Sk first st, ch 1, sc in each of next 7 sts, turn.

Row 3: Sk first st, ch 1, sc in each of next 6 sts, turn.

Row 4: Sk first st, ch 1, sc in each of next 5 sts, turn.

Row 5: Sk first st, ch 1, sc in each of next 4 sts, turn.

Row 6: Sk first st, ch 1, sc in each of next 3 sts, turn.

Row 7: Sk first st, sc in each of next 2 sts, turn,

Row 8: Sk first st, sc in next st, **do not turn.**

Rnd 9: Now working in rnds loosely enough to keep edge from curling, sl st in end of each row down first side, working in starting ch on opposite side of row 1, sl st in each ch across, sl st in end of each row up other side, join in beg sl st. Fasten off.

BORDER

With blue, join with sc in first set of **inside lps** (*see Fig. 7*) on Edge, sc in each set of inside lps around outer edge. Join in beg sc. Fasten off. ∎

RED GOWN

DESIGN BY **JUANITA TURNER**

SKILL LEVEL

INTERMEDIATE

FINISHED SIZE
Fits 11½-inch fashion doll

MATERIALS
- Size 10 crochet cotton:
  200 yds red
- Size 7/1.65mm steel crochet hook
  or size needed to obtain gauge
- Sewing needle
- Matching sewing thread
- Small snaps: 3

GAUGE
10 sc = 1 inch; 11 sc rows = 1 inch

PATTERN NOTES
Join with slip stitch as indicated unless
  otherwise stated.

Chain-3 at beginning of row or round counts as
  first double crochet unless otherwise stated.

INSTRUCTIONS
SKIRT
Row 1: Ch 28 loosely, sc in 2nd ch from hook
  and in each ch across, turn. *(27 sc)*

Row 2: Ch 1, sc in each st across, turn.

Row 3: Ch 1, sc in first st, 2 sc in each of next
  25 sts, sc in last st, turn. *(52 sc)*

Rows 4–10: Ch 1, sc in each st across, turn.

Rnd 11: Now working in rnds, ch 1, sc in each st
  around, to join, insert hook through last sc made
  and 2nd st at beginning of rnd, sl st tog, **turn.**

Rnd 12: Ch 1, working through both
  thicknesses, sc in first 2 overlapped sts, sc
  in each st around, **join** *(see Pattern Notes)*
  in beg sc, turn. *(50 sc)*

Rnd 13: Ch 1, sc in each of first 8 sts, **sc dec** *(see
  Stitch Guide)* in next 2 sts, sc in each of next 30
  sts, sc dec in next 2 sts, sc in each of last 8 sts,
  join in beg sc, turn. *(48 sc)*

Rnd 14: Ch 1, sc in each of first 8 sts, sc dec in
  next 2 sts, sc in each of next 28 sts, sc dec in
  next 2 sts, sc in each of last 8 sts, join in beg sc,
  turn. *(46 sc)*

Rnd 15: Ch 1, sc in each st around, join in beg
  sc, turn.

Rnd 16: Ch 1, sc in each of first 8 sts, sc dec in
  next 2 sts, sc in each of next 26 sts, sc dec in
  next 2 sts, sc in each of last 8 sts, join in beg sc,
  turn. *(44 sc)*

Rnd 17: Ch 1, sc in each st around, join in beg sc,
  turn. Fasten off.

Row 18: Now working in rows for front split, sk
  first 16 sts, join with sc in next st, sc in each of
  last 27 sts, sc in each of 16 sts sk at beg of row,
  turn. *(44 sc)*

Row 19: Ch 1, sc in each of first 6 sts, sc dec in
  next 2 sts, sc in each of next 18 sts, sc dec in
  next 2 sts, sc in each of last 16 sts, turn. *(42 sc)*

Rows 20–30: Ch 1, sc in each st across, turn.

Row 31: Ch 1, sc in each of first 6 sts, sc dec in
  next 2 sts, sc in each of next 17 sts, sc dec in
  next 2 sts, sc in each of last 15 sts, turn. *(40 sc)*

Rows 32–38: Ch 1, sc in each st across, turn.

Row 39: Ch 1, sc in each of first 6 sts, sc dec in next 2 sts, sc in each of next 16 sts, sc dec in next 2 sts, sc in each of last 14 sts, turn. *(38 sc)*

Rows 40–46: Ch 1, sc in each st across, turn.

Row 47: Ch 1, [sc in each of next 11 sts, 2 sc in next st] 3 times, sc in each of last 2 sts, turn. *(41 sc)*

Rows 48–67: Ch 1, sc in each st across, turn.

Row 68: Ch 1, sc in first st, hdc in each of next 39 sts, sc in last st, turn.

Row 69: Ch 1, sc in first st, hdc in each of next 39 sts, sc in last st, **do not turn**.

Rnd 70: Ch 1, 2 sc in end of first row, working around the edges of the split, sc in end of each row to opposite end of row 69, 2 sc in end of row 69, working across row 69, 2 sc in first st, hdc in each st across with 2 sc in last st, join in beg sc. Fasten off.

BODICE

Row 1: Working in starting ch on opposite side of row 1 on Skirt, sk first 12 chs, join with sc in next ch, sc in each of next 2 chs, leaving last 12 chs unworked, turn. *(3 sc)*

Row 2: Ch 1, sc in first st, 2 sc in next st, sc in last st, turn. *(4 sc)*

Row 3: Ch 1, sc in first st, 2 sc in each of next 2 sts, sc in last st, turn. *(6 sc)*

Row 4: Ch 1, sc in each st across, turn.

Row 5: Ch 1, sc in each of first 2 sts, 2 sc in each of next 2 sts, sc in each of last 2 sts, turn. *(8 sc)*

Row 6: Ch 1, sc in first st, 2 sc in next st, sc in each of next 4 sts, 2 sc in next st, sc in last st, turn. *(10 sc)*

Row 7: Ch 1, sc in each st across, turn.

Row 8: Ch 1, sc in each of first 2 sts, 2 sc in each of next 2 sts, sc in each of next 2 sts, 2 sc in each of next 2 sts, sc in each of last 2 sts, turn. *(14 sc)*

Rows 9 & 10: Ch 1, sc in each st across, turn.

Row 11: Ch 3 *(see Pattern Notes)*, dc in same st, 2 dc in each of next 4 sts, sk next st, sc in each of next 2 sts, sk next st, 2 dc in each of last 5 sts, turn. *(22 sts)*

Row 12: Ch 3, dc in each of next 8 sts, sk next st, sc dec in next 2 sts, sk next st, dc in each of last 9 sts, turn. *(19 sts)*

Row 13: Ch 1, sc in each st across. Fasten off.

COLLAR
Row 1: Ch 17, sc in 2nd ch from hook and in each ch across, turn. *(16 sc)*

Row 2: Ch 1, sc in each st across. Fasten off.

LEFT SIDE STRAPS
Row 1: Holding gown with RS facing and working in rem chs in starting ch on opposite side of row 1 of Skirt, join with sc in first ch, sc in each of next 11 chs, working in ends of rows on Bodice, sc in end of each row across to row 10, 2 sc in end of each dc row across to last row, sc in end of last row, ch 10, to attach Collar, sk 10 sts at 1 end of row 2 on Collar, join with sc in next st; working toward other end, sl st in next st, turn.

Row 2: Ch 1, sc in each of 10 chs, sc in each of next 7 sc down side of Bodice, ch 18, sk next 2 sc at same end of Collar, sc in next sc, sl st in last st on Collar, turn.

Row 3: Ch 1, sc in each of 18 chs, sc in each st down Bodice to waist, sc in each of last 12 sts. Fasten off.

RIGHT SIDE STRAPS
Beg with WS facing and counting from other end of Collar, rep rows 1–3 of Left Side Straps.

FINISHING
Sew 1 snap at ends of Collar, 1 snap at waist, and 1 snap about ½ inch below waist.

BLACK, RED & WHITE GOWN
SKILL LEVEL

INTERMEDIATE

FINISHED SIZE
Fits 11½-inch fashion doll

MATERIALS
- Size 10 crochet cotton:
  175 yds black
  40 yds red
  15 yds white
- Size 7/1.65mm steel crochet hook or size needed to obtain gauge
- Sewing needle
- Matching sewing thread
- Small snaps: 4

GAUGE
10 sts = 1 inch; 11 sc rows = 1 inch

PATTERN NOTES
Join with slip stitch as indicated unless otherwise stated.

Chain-3 at beginning of row or round counts as first double crochet unless otherwise stated.

INSTRUCTIONS
BODICE
Row 1: With black, ch 28 loosely, sc in 2nd ch from hook and in each ch across, turn. *(27 sc)*

Rows 2–4: Ch 1, sc in each st across, turn.

Row 5: Ch 1, sc in first st, 2 sc in next st, sc in each of next 5 sts, 2 sc in next st, sc in each st across to last 8 sts, 2 sc in next st, sc in each of next 5 sts, 2 sc in next st, sc in last st, turn. *(31 sc)*

Row 6: Ch 1, sc in each st across, turn.

Row 7: Ch 1, sc in each of first 7 sts, 2 sc in next st, sc in each of next 15 sts, 2 sc in next st, sc in each of last 7 sts, turn. *(33 sc)*

Row 8: Ch 1, sc in each of first 7 sts, 2 sc in each of next 2 sts, sc in each of next 15 sts, 2 sc in each of next 2 sts, sc in each of last 7 sts, turn. *(37 sc)*

Row 9: Ch 1, sc in each st across, turn.

Row 10: Ch 1, sc in each of first 8 sts, 2 sc in next st, sc in each of next 19 sts, 2 sc in next st, sc in each of last 8 sts, turn. *(39 sc)*

Row 11: Ch 1, sc in each st across, turn.

Row 12: Ch 1, sc in each of first 8 sts, 2 sc in next st, sc in each of next 21 sts, 2 sc in next st, sc in each of last 8 sts, turn. *(41 sc)*

Row 13: Ch 1, sc in each of first 15 sts, sk next st, 3 dc in each of next 3 sts, sk next st, sc in next st, sk next st, 3 dc in each of next 3 sts, sk next st, sc in each of last 15 sts, turn. *(49 sts)*

Row 14: Ch 1, sc in each of first 14 sts, sk next st, dc in each of next 8 sts, sk next st, sc in next st, sk next st, dc in each of next 8 sts, sk next st, sc in each of last 14 sts, turn. *(45 sts)*

Row 15: Ch 1, sc in each st across, turn.

Row 16: Ch 1, sc in each of first 22 sts, sk next st, sc in each of last 22 sts, turn. *(44 sc)*

Row 17: Ch 1, sc in each st across, **do not turn.**

Row 18: Working in ends of rows, sc in end of each row across to row 1. **Do not turn or fasten off.**

SKIRT
Row 1: Working in starting ch on opposite side of row 1, ch 1, 2 sc in first ch, sc in each ch across, turn. *(28 sc)*

Row 2: Ch 1, 2 sc in first st, sc in next st, [2 sc in next st, sc in next st] across, turn. *(42 sc)*

Row 3: Ch 1, sc in each st across, turn.

Row 4: Ch 1, 2 sc in first st, sc in each st across to last st, 2 sc in last st, turn. *(44 sc)*

Rows 5–11: Ch 1, sc in each st across, turn.

Row 12: Ch 1, 2 sc in first st, sc in each st across to last st, 2 sc in last st, turn. *(46 sc)*

Rnd 13: Now working in rnds, ch 1, sc in each st around, to join, insert hook in last sc made and in 2nd st at beginning of rnd, sl st tog, turn.

Rnd 14: Ch 1, working through both thicknesses, sc in first 2 overlapped sts, sc in each st around, **join** (*see Pattern Notes*) in beg sc, **turn**. (*44 sc*)

Rnds 15–20: Ch 1, sc in each st around, join in beg sc, turn.

Rnd 21: Ch 1, sc in each of first 10 sts, **sc dec** (*see Stitch Guide*) in next 2 sts, sc in each of next 20 sts, sc dec in next 2 sts, sc in each of last 10 sts, join in beg sc, turn. (*42 sc*)

Rnd 22: Ch 1, sc in each st around, join in beg sc, turn.

Rnd 23: Ch 1, sc in each of first 10 sts, sc dec in next 2 sts, sc in each of next 18 sts, sc dec in next 2 sts, sc in each of last 10 sts, join in beg sc, turn. (*40 sc*)

Rnds 24–26: Ch 1, sc in each st around, join in beg sc, turn.

Rnd 27: Ch 1, sc in each of first 10 sts, sc dec in next 2 sts, sc in each of next 16 sts, sc dec in next 2 sts, sc in each of last 10 sts, join in beg sc, turn. (*38 sc*)

Rnd 28: Ch 1, sc in each st around, join in beg sc, turn.

Rnd 29: Ch 1, sc in each of first 10 sts, sc dec in next 2 sts, sc in each of next 14 sts, sc dec in next 2 sts, sc in each of last 10 sts, join in beg sc, turn. (*36 sc*)

Rnds 30–32: Ch 1, sc in each st around, join in beg sc, turn.

Rnd 33: Ch 1, sc in each of first 9 sts, sc dec in next 2 sts, sc in each of next 14 sts, sc dec in next 2 sts, sc in each of last 9 sts, join in beg sc, turn. (*34 sc*)

Rnd 34: Ch 1, sc in each st around, join in beg sc, turn.

Rnd 35: Ch 1, sc in each of first 9 sts, sc dec in next 2 sts, sc in each of next 12 sts, sc dec in next 2 sts, sc in each of last 9 sts, join in beg sc, turn. Fasten off. (*32 sc*)

Row 36: Now working in rows, holding Skirt upside down with back facing, count from center back toward left and join black with sc in 14th st (*this is on right leg at front of doll*), sc in each of next 29 sts, leaving last 2 sts unworked, turn, **do not join**. (*30 sc*)

Row 37: Ch 1, sc in each of first 26 sts, sc dec in next 2 sts, sc in each of last 2 sts, turn. (*29 sc*)

Rows 38–40: Ch 1, sc in each st across, turn.

Row 41: Ch 1, sc in each of first 12 sts, 2 sc in each of next 2 sts, sc in each of last 15 sts, turn. (*31 sc*)

Row 42: Ch 1, sc in each st across, turn.

Row 43: Ch 1, sc in each of first 2 sts, sc dec in next 2 sts, sc in each of next 8 sts, 2 sc in each of next 2 sts, sc in each of last 17 sts, turn. (*32 sc*)

Rows 44–50: Ch 1, sc in each st across, turn.

Row 51: Ch 1, sc in each of first 2 sts, sc dec in next 2 sts, sc in each of next 24 sts, 2 sc in next st, sc in each of last 3 sts, turn. (*32 sc*)

Rows 52–58: Ch 1, sc in each st across, turn.

Row 59: Ch 1, sc in each of first 2 sts, sc dec in next 2 sts, sc in each of next 23 sts, 2 sc in each of next 2 sts, sc in each of last 3 sts, turn. (*33 sc*)

Rows 60–66: Ch 1, sc in each st across, turn.

Row 67: Ch 1, sc in each st across to last st, 2 sc in last st, **do not turn**. (*34 sc*)

Row 68: Working in ends of rows, ch 1, 2 sc in end of row 67, sc in end of each row across to rnd 35, sl st in next st on rnd 35, turn.

Row 69: Ch 1, sc in each st across row 68, ch 1, 2 sc in ch-1 sp, sc in each st across row 67 with 2 sc in last st, **do not turn**.

Row 70: Ch 1, 2 sc in end of row 69, sc in end of each row across to rnd 35, sl st in next st on rnd 35, turn. Fasten off.

TRIM

Row 1: Join red in last sl st on Skirt, working in row 70 across front of split on Skirt, sc in each of next 10 sts, hdc in each of next 10 sts, dc in each st across, turn.

Row 2: Ch 1, sc in each dc and in each hdc and sl st in each sc across, sl st in joining sl st, turn.

Row 3: Ch 1, sk first st, sl st in each of next 4 sts, sc in each st across to last st, 2 sc in last st, **do not turn.**

Row 4: Working in ends of rows 1–3, ch 1, 2 sc in end of row 3, sc in end of row 2, 3 sc evenly spaced across dc at end of row 1, sc in each st across bottom of Skirt, turn.

Row 5: Ch 1, sk first st, sl st in each st across, ch 1, working up Split edge, sc in each st up to rnd 35, sl st in next worked st on rnd 35, turn.

Row 6: Ch 1, sk first st, sl st in each sc across to bottom edge of Skirt. Fasten off.

COLLAR

Rnd 1: With white, ch 55, sl st in first ch to form ring, ch 1, sc in each of first 9 chs, hdc in each of next 9 chs, dc in each of next 9 chs, 3 dc in next ch, dc in each of next 9 chs, hdc in each of next 9 chs, sc in each of last 9 chs, join in beg sc. (57 sts)

Rnd 2: Ch 1, sc in each of first 8 sts, hdc in each of next 9 sts, dc in each of next 10 sts, 2 dc in next st, dc in next st, 2 dc in next st, dc in each of next 10 sts, hdc in each of next 9 sts, sc in each of last 8 sts, join. (59 sts)

Rnd 3: Ch 1, sc in each st around, join in beg sc. Fasten off.

Rnd 4: Working in starting ch on opposite side of rnd 1, join red with sc in first ch, sc in each of next 8 chs, hdc in each of next 9 chs, dc in each of next 9 chs, 3 dc in next ch, dc in each of next 9 chs, hdc in each of next 9 chs, sc in each of last 9 chs, join in beg sc. (57 sts)

Rnd 5: Ch 1, sc in each of first 8 sts, hdc in each of next 9 sts, dc in each of next 10 sts, 2 dc in next st, dc in next st, 2 dc in next st, dc in each of next 10 sts, hdc in each of next 9 sts, sc in each of last 8 sts, join in beg sc. (59 sts)

Rnd 6: Ch 1, sc in each st around, join in beg sc. Fasten off.

FINISHING

1. With row 18 overlapping rem side, sew 3 snaps evenly sp across back opening of Bodice, sew 1 snap at ends of row 7 on Skirt.

2. Holding Collar above Bodice with wide side of Collar at left and white Collar stripe next to Bodice, sew 15 sts on rnd 3 of Collar to center 15 sts at top front of Bodice. ■

Garden **Room**

SKILL LEVEL

EASY

FINISHED SIZE
7½ inches long

MATERIALS
- Medium (worsted) weight yarn:
  2 oz/100yds/57g rose
- Sizes F/5/3.75mm and G/6/4mm
  crochet hooks or size needed to
  obtain gauge
- Stitch marker

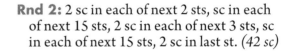

GAUGE
Size G hook: 4 sc = 1 inch; 4 sc rows = 1 inch

PATTERN NOTES
Work in continuous rounds, do not turn
  or join unless otherwise stated.

Mark first stitch of each round.

SPECIAL STITCH
Fasten off invisibly: Leaving 6-inch end, cut yarn,
  insert hook through first st of rnd and pull end
  through st and lp on hook, tighten lp to match
  size of other sts, blending end with lps of next
  st, pull end through to WS of work and secure
  in back of sts.

INSTRUCTIONS
CUSHION
OVAL
MAKE 3.
Rnd 1: With size G hook, ch 18, 2 sc in 2nd ch
  from hook, sc in each of next 15 chs, 3 sc in
  last ch, working on opposite side ch, sc in
  each of next 15 chs, sc in last ch, **do not join
  rnds**. (36 sc)

Rnd 2: 2 sc in each of next 2 sts, sc in each
  of next 15 sts, 2 sc in each of next 3 sts, sc
  in each of next 15 sts, 2 sc in last st. (42 sc)

Rnd 3: 2 sc in each of next 3 sts, sc in each
  of next 18 sts, 2 sc in each of next 3 sts, sc
  in each of next 18 sts. (48 sc)

Rnd 4: *2 sc in next st, [sc in next st, 2 sc in
  next st] twice, sc in each of next 18 sts, rep
  from *. (54 sc)

Rnd 5: *2 sc in next st, [sc in next st, 2 sc in
  next st] 3 times, sc in each of next 20 sts, rep
  from *. (62 sc)

Rnd 6: *Sc in next st, 2 sc in next st, [sc in each
  of next 2 sts, 2 sc in next st] 3 times, sc in each
  of next 19 sts, rep from *, sc in next st, sl st in
  next sc. Fasten off.

FINISHING
Holding all Ovals tog with 2 outer pieces having
  WS tog, working through all thicknesses, with
  size F hook, join with sl st in any st on last rnd,
  working just loosely enough so edge will lie
  flat, sl st in each st around. **Fasten off invisibly**
  (see Special Stitch).

CHAISE LOUNGE
SKILL LEVEL

EASY

FINISHED SIZE
9½ inches long

MATERIALS
- Medium (worsted) weight yarn:
  6 oz/300yds/170g white
- Sizes F/5/3.75mm and H/8/5mm
  crochet hooks or size needed
  to obtain gauge
- Tapestry needle
- Cardboard
- Craft glue

GAUGE
Size H hook: 4 sc = 1 inch; 4 sc rows = 1 inch

Size F hook: 9 sts = 2 inches; 4 fpdc rows = 2 inches

PATTERN NOTES
Join with slip stitch as indicated unless
otherwise stated.

Chain-3 at beginning of row or round counts as
first double crochet unless otherwise stated.

SPECIAL STITCH
Fasten off invisibly: Leaving 6-inch end, cut yarn,
insert hook through first st of rnd and pull end
through st and lp on hook, tighten lp to match
size of other sts, blending end with lps of next
st, pull end through to WS of work and secure
in back of sts.

PATTERNS
BASKET WEAVE
[**Fpdc** (*see Stitch Guide*) around next st, **bpdc** (*see
Stitch Guide*) around next st] across or around,
always alternating front and back post sts. The
end of some dec rnds will be an exception to
this alternating rule.

BASKET WEAVE ROW
Ends with dc worked under turning ch of
previous row, turn.

To **work under a turning ch** at the end of a
post st row, yo, insert hook in sp between

last st and turning ch on previous row, yo, pull
through, [yo pull through 2 lps on hook] twice.

INSTRUCTIONS
SEAT CORE
Row 1: With size H hook, ch 10, sc in 2nd ch
from hook and in each ch across, turn.

Row should measure about 2¼ inches across.

Row 2: Working in **back lps** (*see Stitch Guide*)
only, ch 1, sc in each st across, turn.

Rows 3–254: Rep row 2. At end of last row,
fasten off.

Glue first 20 rows to 2 x 5 inch piece of
cardboard. Firmly roll up Seat Core around
first 20 rows, tacking or gluing layers tog as
you work, rolled piece should measure 3¼ x
7¼ inches, sl st last row to rem lps of matching
ridge on outside of piece. Fasten off.

SIDES & FRONT
Row 1: With size F hook, ch 19, dc in 4th ch
from hook (*first 3 chs count as first dc*), dc in
each ch across, turn. (*17 dc*)

Side should measure about 3¾ inches wide.

Rows 2–4: **Ch 3** (*see Pattern Notes*), work
Basket Weave Pattern across (*see Patterns*).

Row 5: Ch 3, work Pattern across next 8 sts,
leaving last 8 sts unworked. (*9 sts*)

Front should measure about 2¼ inches wide.

Rows 6–30: Ch 3, work Pattern across, turn.

Row 31: Ch 3, work Pattern across, turn,

Row 32: Ch 10, dc in 4th ch from hook, dc in
each rem ch across, [bpdc around next st, fpdc
around next st] across, ending with dc under
turning ch, turn. (*17 sts*)

Side should measure about 3¾ inches wide.

Rows 33–35: Ch 3, work Pattern across. At end
of last row, fasten off.

FIRST BACK

Row 1: With RS of last row facing, with F hook, sk first 9 sts, join with sl st in next st (*see Fig. 1*), ch 10, turn so WS of row 35 is facing, dc in 4th ch from hook, dc in each rem ch of ch 10, fpdc around dc post st that joining sl st was worked in, [bpdc around next st, fpdc around next st] across, ending with dc under turning ch, turn. (*18 sts*)

Row 2: Ch 3, [fpdc around next st, bpdc around next st] across to last 3 sts, fpdc around next st, bptr around next st, 2 tr under turning ch, turn. (*19 sts*)

Row 3: Ch 4, tr in sp between turning ch and tr on last row, fptr around next tr, bptr around next st, fptr around next st, work Basket Weave Pattern in dc across. (*20 sts*)

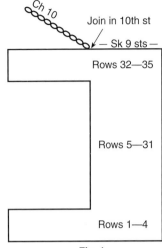

Fig. 1
Victorian Boudoir
Chaise Lounge
Back Diagram

Row 4: Ch 3, fpdc around next st, work Pattern across to last 4 sts, bptr around next st, fptr around next st, bptr around next st, 2 tr under turning ch, turn. *(21 sts)*

Row 5: Ch 3, fpdc around next st, work Pattern across.

Back should measure 4½ inches.

Row 6: Ch 3, fpdc around next st, work Pattern across lo last 5 sts, bptr around next st, fptr around next st, bptr around next st, sk next st, tr under turning ch, turn. *(20 sts)*

Row 7: Ch 4, sk next tr, fptr around next st, bptr around next st, fptr around next st, work Pattern across. *(19 sts)*

Row 8: Ch 4, fpdc around next st, work Pattern across to last 3 sts, bptr around next st, sk next st, tr under turning ch, turn. *(18 sts)*

Row 9: Ch 3, work Pattern across. At end of row on First Back only, **do not turn.** Fasten off.

FINISHING
Fold piece holding row 1 of Sides & Front behind row 9 of First Back, sew last 9 sts of row 9 to matching lps across bottom of row 1.

2ND BACK
Row 1: With size F hook, ch 20, dc in 4th ch from hook, dc in each ch across, turn. *(18 dc)*

Rows 2–9: Rep rows 2–9 of First Back.

BACK EDGING
Matching first and last rows, hold 2nd Back behind First Back *(see Fig. 2),* working through both thicknesses, with size F hook, join with sl st in end of seam where First Back was sewn to Sides & Front, sc in first unworked st on Back, sc in next st, sk next 2 sts, 5 dc in next st, sk next 2 sts, sc in next st, sk next 2 sts, working across ends of rows on Back pieces, 5 dc in end of first row, [sc in next row, 5 dc in next row] 4 times, working down other side of Back, sk next 2 sts, sc in next st, sk next 2 sts, 5 dc in next st, sk next 2 sts, sc in each of next 2 sts, sl st in sp between first row of Back and last row of Side. Fasten off.

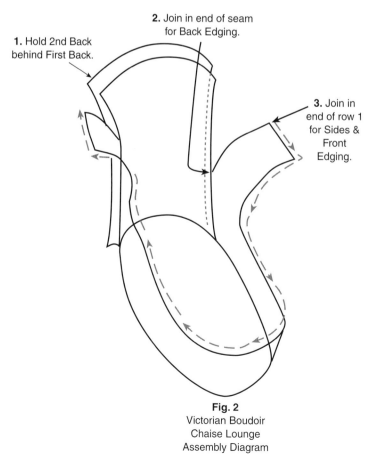

1. Hold 2nd Back behind First Back.

2. Join in end of seam for Back Edging.

3. Join in end of row 1 for Sides & Front Edging.

Fig. 2
Victorian Boudoir
Chaise Lounge
Assembly Diagram

SIDES & FRONT EDGING

Working across top edge of Sides & Front, with size F hook, join with sc in end of row 1, 2 sc in end of each of next 4 rows, sc in each unworked st across row 4, sk end of row 5, sc in end of next 25 rows, sk next row, sc in each rem lp of ch-10 made at end of row 31, 2 sc in end of each of next 3 rows, 3 sc in last row. Fasten off.

BOTTOM EDGING

Working in ends of rows around bottom edge of assembled Sides, Front and through both layers of Backs, with size F hook, join with sc in end of row 9 on Back, 5 dc in next row, [sc in next row, 5 dc in next row] around, join in beg sc. Fasten off.

FINISHING

1. Sew rem side edges at bottom half of 2nd Back to bottom half of First Back.

2. Insert Seat Core through center of assembled Sides, Front and Back, glue or invisibly tack top edge of Seat in place.

3. Roll flaps on each Side down to form armrests (see Fig. 3), tack rolled Flaps in place.

Fig. 3
Victorian Boudoir
Chaise Lounge
Side Diagram

4. Place Lounge Cushion over Seat Core.

TABLE

SKILL LEVEL
INTERMEDIATE

FINISHED SIZE
3½ inches across Top and 3 inches tall

MATERIALS
- Medium (worsted) weight yarn: 2 oz/100yds/57g white
- Size F/5/3.75mm crochet hook or size needed to obtain gauge
- Tapestry needle
- Plastic margarine lid
- Fabric stiffener
- Craft glue

4 MEDIUM

GAUGE
4 sc = 1 inch; 4 sc rows = 1 inch

PATTERN NOTES
Join with slip stitch as indicated unless otherwise stated.

Chain-3 at beginning of row or round counts as first double crochet unless otherwise stated.

To stiffen crochet work, the following starching solutions are recommended; test desired solution on a swatch to ensure correct stiffness and to make sure yarn doesn't become over coated or discolored:

Clear drying craft glue: Dilute 2 parts glue to desired consistency with 1 part water, let this solution air dry only.

Powdered laundry starch: Double the amount of starch for heavy stiffness in directions, then prepare starch according to the hot starch method in package directions.

Old Fashioned sugar starch: Mix ½ cup sugar with ¼ cup water in pan over very low heat, stirring until mixture becomes clear. Be sure it does not boil, remove from heat, allow solution to cool before using. Apply an acrylic, non-glossy glaze when dry.

Soak crochet work in solution, then lightly press out excess moisture, shape and let dry completely.

Speedier drying: Warm an oven to 150–200 degrees, **turn off oven** and place crochet inside. If needed, remove crochet, re-warm oven and replace crochet until dry.

SPECIAL STITCH
Fasten off invisibly: Leaving 6-inch end, cut yarn, insert hook through first st of rnd and pull end through st and lp on hook, tighten lp to match size of other sts, blending end with lps of next st, pull end through to WS of work and secure in back of sts.

PATTERNS
BASKET WEAVE
[**Fpdc** (see Stitch Guide) around next st, **bpdc** (see Stitch Guide) around next st] across or around, always alternating front and back posts sts. The end of some dec rnds will be an exception to this alternating rule.

BASKET WEAVE RNDS
Will sk over the first st of previous rnd and beg in the 2nd st, the last post st of the rnd will be worked around the sk st at beg unless otherwise stated in the instructions.

INSTRUCTIONS
TABLE
BASE
Rnd 1: Ch 12, sl st in first ch to form ring, **ch 3** (see Pattern Notes), dc in same ch, 2 dc in each ch around, **join** (see Pattern Notes) in 3rd ch of beg ch 3. (24 dc)

Rnds 2 & 3: Sl st in next st, **fpsc** (see Stitch Guide) around st on rnd below, ch 2, **Basket Weave Pattern** (see Patterns) around, join in 2nd ch of beg ch-2.

Rnd 4: Sl st tightly in each st around.

Rnd 5: Working in **back lps** (see Stitch Guide) of sl sts on last rnd, ch 1, sc in first st, sk next st, 4 dc in next st, sk next st, [sc in next st, sk next st, 4 dc in next, sk next st] around, join in beg sc. Fasten off.

BOTTOM RIM
Rnd 1: Working in starting ch on opposite side of rnd 1 on Base, join with sc in any ch, sc in next ch, 2 sc in next ch, [sc in each of next 2 chs, 2 sc in next ch] around, join in beg sc. (16 sc)

Rnd 2: Ch 1, sc in first st, sk next st, 5 dc in next st, sk next st, [sc in next st, sk next st, 5 dc in next st, sk next st] around, join in beg sc. Fasten off.

TOP
MAKE 2.
Rnd 1: Ch 2, 6 sc in 2nd ch from hook, **do not join rnds**. (6 sc)

Rnd 2: 2 sc in each st around. (12 sc)

Rnd 3: [Sc in next st, 2 sc in next st] around. (18 sc)

Rnd 4: [Sc in each of next 2 sts, 2 sc in next st] around. (24 sc)

Rnd 5: [Sc in each of next 3 sts, 2 sc in next st] around. (30 sc)

Rnd 6: [Sc in each of next 4 sts, 2 sc in next st] around, join in beg sc. Fasten off.

Using crocheted piece as pattern, trace and cut 1 circle from plastic lid. Trim about ⅛ inch from edge of plastic circle.

Hold both pieces with WS tog, working through all thicknesses, join with sl st in any st of last rnd, working just loosely enough so edge will lie flat, sl st in each st around, inserting plastic circle before closing. Fasten off invisibly *(see Special Stitch)*.

FINISHING
Apply stiffener to Base and Top, shape and allow to dry completely *(see Pattern Notes)*. Glue Top to Base.

WICKER PLANT URN
SKILL LEVEL

INTERMEDIATE

FINISHED SIZE
2¼ inches tall

MATERIALS
- Medium (worsted) weight yarn: 2 oz/100yds/57g white
- Size F/5/3.75mm crochet hook or size needed to obtain gauge
- Small bunch artificial flowers
- Fabric stiffener

MEDIUM

GAUGE
4 sc = 1 inch; 4 sc rows = 1 inch

PATTERN NOTES
Join with slip stitch as indicated unless otherwise stated.

Chain-3 at beginning of row or round counts as first double crochet unless otherwise stated.

To stiffen crochet work, the following starching solutions are recommended; test desired solution on a swatch to ensure correct stiffness and to make sure yarn doesn't become over coated or discolored:

Clear drying craft glue: Dilute 2 parts glue to desired consistency with 1 part water, let this solution air dry only.

Powdered laundry starch: Double the amount of starch for heavy stiffness in directions, then prepare starch according to the hot starch method in package directions.

Old Fashioned sugar starch: Mix ½ cup sugar with ¼ cup water in pan over very low heat, stirring until mixture becomes clear. Be sure it does not boil, remove from heat, allow solution to cool a little before using. Apply an acrylic, non-glossy glaze when dry.

Soak crochet work in solution, then lightly press out excess moisture, shape and let dry completely.

Speedier drying: Warm an oven to 150–200 degrees, **turn off oven** and place crochet inside. If needed, remove crochet, re-warm oven and replace crochet until dry.

SPECIAL STITCH
Fasten off invisibly: Leaving 6-inch end, cut yarn, insert hook through first st of rnd and pull end through st and lp on hook, tighten lp to match size of other sts, blending end with lps of next st, pull end through to WS of work and secure in back of sts.

PATTERNS
BASKET WEAVE

[**Fpdc** (*see Stitch Guide*) around next st, **bpdc** (*see Stitch Guide*) around next st] across or around, always alternating front and back posts sts. The end of some dec rnds will be an exception to this alternating rule.

BASKET WEAVE RNDS

Will sk over the first st of previous rnd and beg in the 2nd st, the last post st of the rnd will be worked around the sk st at beg unless otherwise stated in the instructions.

INSTRUCTIONS
URN

Rnd 1: Ch 2, 6 sc in 2nd ch from hook, **do not join this rnd**. (*6 sc*)

Rnd 2: 2 sc in each st around. (*12 sc*)

Rnd 3: Working in **back lps** (*see Stitch Guide*), sl st in next st, **ch 3** (*see Pattern Notes*), dc in same st, 2 dc in each st around, **join** (*see Pattern Notes*) in 3rd ch of beg ch-3. (*24 dc*)

Rnds 4 & 5: Ch 1, sk first st on last rnd, **fpsc** (*see Stitch Guide*) around next st, ch 2, **bpdc** (*see Stitch Guide*) around next st, **Basket Weave Pattern** (*see Pattern*) around, working last post st around sk st at beg of rnd, join in 2nd ch of beg ch-2.

TOP EDGE

Rnd 6: Ch 1, sc in first st, sk next st, 5 dc in next st, sk next st, [sc in next st, sk next st, 5 dc in next st, sk next st] around, join in beg sc. Fasten off.

BOTTOM EDGE

Hold bottom of Urn pointing up, working in rem front lps of rnd 2 on Urn, join with sc in any st, sk next st, 5 dc in next st, [sc in next st, sk next st, 5 dc in next st] around, join in beg sc. Fasten off.

FINISHING

Apply desired stiffener, shape and allow to dry completely. Place flowers in Urn.

LARGE ROUND RUG
SKILL LEVEL

INTERMEDIATE

FINISHED SIZE

6 inches across

MATERIALS

- Medium (worsted) weight yarn: 1 oz/50yds/28g green
- Size G/6/4mm crochet hook or size needed to obtain gauge

GAUGE

4 sc = 1 inch; 2 dc rows = 1 inch

PATTERN NOTES

Join with slip stitch as indicated unless otherwise stated.

Chain-3 at beginning of row or round counts as first double crochet unless otherwise stated.

INSTRUCTIONS
RUG

Rnd 1: Ch 2, 6 sc in 2nd ch from hook, **join** *(see Pattern Notes)* in beg sc. *(6 sc)*

Rnd 2: Ch 3 *(see Pattern Note)*, 3 dc in each st around, 2 dc in same st as beg ch-3, join in 3rd ch of beg ch-3. *(18 dc)*

Rnd 3: Ch 3, 2 dc in each st around, dc in same st as beg ch-3, join in 3rd ch of beg ch-3. *(36 dc)*

Rnd 4: Ch 3, dc in next st, [2 dc in next st, dc in each of next 2 sts] around, ending with 2 dc in last st, join in 3rd ch of beg ch-3. *(48 dc)*

Rnd 5: Ch 3, [dc in each of next 3 sts, 2 dc in next st] around, ending with dc in same st as beg ch-3, join in 3rd ch of beg ch-3. *(60 dc)*

Rnd 6: Ch 1, sc in first st, ch 5, sl st in top of sc just made, [sc in next st, ch 5, sl st in top of sc just made] around, join in beg sc. Fasten off.

AFGHAN
SKILL LEVEL

INTERMEDIATE

FINISHED SIZE
6½ inches long, excluding Fringe

MATERIALS
- Fine (sport) weight yarn:
  1 oz/100yds/28g white
- Size E/4/3.5mm crochet hook
  or size needed to obtain gauge

MEDIUM

GAUGE
5 dc = 1 inch; 3 dc rows = 1 inch

PATTERN NOTE
Chain-3 at beginning of row or round counts as first double crochet unless otherwise stated.

INSTRUCTIONS
AFGHAN

Row 1: Ch 25, 2 dc in 4th ch from hook, [sk next ch, 2 dc in next ch] across, ending with dc in last ch, turn.

Rows 2–19: Working in sps between sts, **ch 3** *(see Pattern Note)*, sk next sp between sts, [2 dc in next sp, sk next sp] across, ending with dc in last st, turn. At end of last row, fasten off.

FRINGE
Cut 2½-inch strand yarn, fold in half, pull through st, pull ends through fold. Pull ends to tighten.

Attach Fringe in each st across each short end of Afghan as shown in photo.

HEART PILLOW
SKILL LEVEL

INTERMEDIATE

FINISHED SIZE
2¾ inches across

MATERIALS
- Medium (worsted) weight yarn:
  1 oz/50yds/28g each pink and white
- Size F/5/3.75mm crochet hook
  or size needed to obtain gauge
- Fiberfill

MEDIUM

GAUGE
4 sc = 1 inch; 2 dc rows = 1 inch

INSTRUCTIONS
PILLOW
SIDE
MAKE 2.
Rnd 1: Ch 2, 6 sc in 2nd ch from hook, **do not join rnds.** *(6 sc)*

Rnd 2: 2 sc in each st around. *(12 sc)*

Rnd 3: Sc in next st, dc in next st, 2 tr in each of next 2 sts, [3 dc in next st, 2 hdc in next st] twice, 3 dc in next st, 2 tr in each of next 2 sts, dc in next st, join in beg sc. Fasten off.

TRIM
Hold both pieces WS tog, working through both thicknesses and in **back lps** *(see Stitch Guide)*, join white with sc in first st on last rnd, ch 1, (sc, ch 1) in each st around, stuff before closing, join with sl st in beg sc. Fasten off.

FLOOR LAMP
SKILL LEVEL
INTERMEDIATE

FINISHED SIZE
9 inches tall

MATERIALS
- Medium (worsted) weight yarn: 2 oz/100yds/57g white
- Sizes E/4/3.5mm and F/5/3.75mm crochet hooks or size needed to obtain gauge
- Tapestry needle
- Fiberfill
- Fabric stiffener
- Acrylic, non-glossy glaze
- Craft glue

4 MEDIUM

GAUGE
Size F hook: 4 sc = 1 inch; 5 post st rows = 2 inches

Size E hook: 5 sc = 1 inch; 9 sc rows = 2 inches

PATTERN NOTES
Join with slip stitch as indicated unless otherwise stated.

Chain-3 at beginning of row or round counts as first double crochet unless otherwise stated.

To stiffen crochet work, the following starching solutions are recommended; test desired solution on a swatch to ensure correct stiffness and to make sure yarn doesn't become over coated or discolored:

Clear drying craft glue: Dilute 2 parts glue to desired consistency with 1 part water, let this solution air dry only.

Powdered laundry starch: Double the amount of starch for heavy stiffness in directions, then prepare starch according to the hot starch method in package directions.

Old Fashioned sugar starch: Mix ½ cup sugar with ¼ cup water in pan over very low heat, stirring until mixture becomes clear, be sure it does not boil, remove from heat, allow solution to cool before using. Apply an acrylic, non-glossy glaze when dry.

Soak crochet work in solution, then lightly press out excess moisture, shape and let dry completely.

Speedier drying: Warm an oven to 150-200 degrees, **turn off oven** and place crochet inside. If needed, remove crochet, re-warm oven and replace crochet until dry.

SPECIAL STITCH
Fasten off invisibly: Leaving 6-inch end, cut yarn, insert hook through first st of rnd and pull end through st and lp on hook, tighten lp to match size of other sts, blending end with lps of next st, pull end through to WS of work and secure in back of sts.

PATTERNS
BASKET WEAVE
[**Fpdc** (*see Stitch Guide*) around next st, **bpdc** (*see Stitch Guide*) around next st] across or around, always alternating front and back posts sts. The end of some dec rnds will be an exception to this alternating rule.

BASKET WEAVE RNDS
Will sk over the first st of previous rnd and beg in the 2nd st, the last post st of the rnd will be worked around the sk st at beg unless otherwise stated in the instructions.

INSTRUCTIONS
LAMP
BASE & POST
Rnd 1: With size F hook, ch 28, sl st in first ch to form ring, **ch 3** (*see Pattern Notes*), dc in each ch around, join in 3rd ch of beg ch-3. (*28 dc*)

Rnd 2: Ch 1, **fpsc** (*see Stitch Guide*) around first st, ch 2, **bpdc** (*see Stitch Guide*) around next st. **Basket Weave Pattern** (*see Patterns*) in each of next 4 sts, sk next st, [continue Pattern in each of next 6 sts, sk next st] 3 times, join in 2nd ch of beg ch-2. (*24 sts*)

Rnd 3: Ch 1, sk first st on last rnd, fpsc around next st, ch 2, bpdc around next st, fpdc around next st, bpdc around next st, sk next 2 sts, *[fpdc around next st, bpdc around next st] twice, sk next 2 sts, rep from * twice, sk only 1 st at end of last rep, join in 2nd ch of beg ch-2. (*16 sts*)

Rnd 4: Ch 1, sk first st, fpsc around next st, ch 2, bpdc around next st, fpdc around next st, bpdc around next st, sk next 2 sts, [fpdc around next st, bpdc around next st] twice, sk next 2 sts, fpdc around next st, bpdc around next st, sk next st and sk st at beg of rnd, join in 2nd ch of beg ch-2. (*10 sts*)

Rnds 5–21: Ch 1, sk first st on last rnd, fpsc around next st, ch 2, bpdc around next st, Basket Weave Pattern around, working last post st around sk st at beg of rnd, join in 2nd ch of beg ch-2. Stuff Post only as you work. At end of last rnd, **do not fasten off.**

BULB
Rnd 1: Working in **back lps** (*see Stitch Guide*) *only* of rnd 21, with size E hook, ch 1, sc in each st around, do not join rnds. (*10 sc*)

Rnd 2: 2 sc in each st around. (*20 sc*)

Rnd 3: [Sc in next st, 2 sc in next st] around. (*30 sc*)

Rnds 4–7: Sc in each st around. Stuff and shape.

Rnds 8 & 9: [**Sc dec** (*see Stitch Guide*) in next 2 sts] around. At end of last rnd, sc in last st, join in beg sc. Fasten off. (*8 sc at end of last rnd*)

Sew opening at top of Bulb closed.

BASE EDGING
Rnd 1: Working in starting ch on opposite side of rnd 1 on Base & Post, with size F hook, join in any ch, sl st loosely in each ch around, **do not join this rnd.** (*28 sl sts*)

Rnd 2: [Sc in next st, sk next st, 4 dc in next st, sk next st] around, join in beg sc. Fasten off.

LAMP SHADE
Rnd 1: With size F hook, ch 20, sl st in first ch to form ring, ch 3, dc in same ch as ch 3, 2 dc in each ch around, join in 3rd ch of beg ch-3. (*40 dc*)

Rnds 2–4: Ch 1, sk first st on last rnd, fpsc around next st, ch 2, bpdc around next st, work Basket Weave Pattern around, working last post st around sk st at beg of rnd, join in 2nd ch of beg ch-2.

Rnd 5: Ch 1, [sc in next st, sk next st, 5 dc in next st, sk next st] around, join in beg sc. Fasten off.

TOP EDGING
Working in starting ch on opposite side of rnd 1 on Lamp Shade, with size F hook, join with sc in any ch, sk next ch, 5 dc in next ch, sk next ch, [sc in next ch, sk next ch, 5 dc in next ch, sk next ch] around, join in beg sc. Fasten off.

FINISHING
1. Apply stiffener to all pieces (*see Pattern Notes*).

2. While still damp, shape Base, push Post down inside Base to match bottom edge.

3. Shape Bulb and Lamp Shade and allow to dry completely.

4. Place Lamp Shade over Bulb as shown in photo. ■

Sofa & Chair

DESIGN BY **MARY LAYFIELD**

SKILL LEVEL

INTERMEDIATE

FINISHED SIZES

Sofa: 4½ inches tall x 9½ inches long

Chair: 4½ inches tall x 4½ inches wide

MATERIALS

- Medium (worsted) weight yarn: 8 oz/400 yds/227g green

- Size G/6/4mm crochet hook or size needed to obtain gauge
- Tapestry needle
- Large sheet foam board or cardboard
- Fiberfill
- Craft glue

GAUGE

4 sc = 1 inch; 1 sc rows = 1 inch

PATTERN NOTES

Chain-2 at beginning of row or round counts as first half double crochet unless otherwise stated.

Chain-3 at beginning of row or round counts as first double crochet unless otherwise stated.

INSTRUCTIONS

SOFA
FRONT

Row 1: Ch 32, sc in 2nd ch from hook and in each ch across, turn. *(31 sc)*

Rows 2–32: Ch 1, sc in each st across, turn. At end of last row, fasten off.

INSIDE ARM
MAKE 2.

Row 1: Ch 12, sc in 2nd ch from hook, sc in each ch across, turn. *(11 sc)*

Rows 2–6: Ch 1, sc in each st across, turn.

Row 7: Ch 1, sc in each of first 3 sts leaving rem sts unworked, turn.

Row 8: Ch 1, sk first st, sc in each of last 2 sts, turn.

Row 9: Ch 1, **sc dec** *(see Stitch Guide)* in first 2 sts. Fasten off.

OUTSIDE ARM
MAKE 2.

Row 1: Ch 14, sc in 2nd ch from hook and in each ch across, turn. *(13 sc)*

Rows 2–13: Ch 1, sc in each st across, turn.

Row 14: Ch 1, sc in each of first 5 sts leaving rem sts unworked, turn.

Row 15: Ch 1, sk first st, sc in each st across, turn.

Row 16: Ch 1, sc in each of first 4 sts leaving rem st unworked, turn.

Row 17: Ch 1, sc in each of first 2 sts, sc dec in last 2 sts, turn.

Row 18: Ch 1, sc dec in first 2 sts. Fasten off.

BOTTOM

Row 1: Ch 32, sc in 2nd ch from hook and in each ch across, turn. *(31 sc)*

Row 2: Ch 2 *(see Pattern Notes)*, hdc in each st across, turn.

Row 3: Ch 1, sc in each st across, turn.

Rows 4–9: [Rep rows 2 and 3 alternately] 3 times. At end of last row, fasten off.

BACK

Row 1: Ch 33, sc in 2nd ch from hook and in each ch across, turn. *(32 sc)*

Row 2: Ch 3 *(see Pattern Notes)*, dc in each st across, turn.

Row 3: Ch 1, sc in each st across, turn.

Rows 4–10: [Rep rows 2 and 3 alternately] 4 times, ending last rep with row 2. At end of last row, fasten off.

ASSEMBLY

1. From foam board, cut 1 each of the following pieces:

1½ x 8½ inches for seat front

2½ x 8½ inches for seat

2¼ x 8½ inches for seat back

2¾ x 8½ inches for bottom

3¾ x 8½ inches for back

2. Using crochet pieces as pattern cut 2 Outside Arm pieces from foam board.

3. Matching front and top edges, glue 1 Inside Arm to 1 side of foam board and 1 Outside Arm to other side of same board, whipstitch front and top edges tog. Rep with 2nd set of Arms.

4. Aligning edge of row 1 on crochet Front to 1 long edge, glue Seat Front over crochet piece, glue Seat to Front 1 row over front Seat Front, glue Seat Back 1 row over front Seat Front, glue Bottom and Back to matching foam board pieces *(see Fig. 1)*.

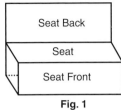

Fig. 1
Garden Room
Sofa Assembly

5. Sew all crocheted pieces tog easing to fit over foam board, sew Arms to assembled Seat and Back.

SOFA COVERING
INSIDE PIECE
Row 1: Ch 40, sc in 2nd ch from hook and in each ch across, turn. *(39 sc)*

Row 2: Ch 4 *(counts as first dc and ch-1)*, sk next st, dc in next st, [ch 1, sk next st, c in next st] across, turn.

Row 3: Ch 1, sc in each st and in each ch across, turn.

FIRST LEG
Row 4: Ch 1, sc in each of first 3 sts leaving rem sts unworked, turn. *(3 sc)*

Rows 5 & 6: Ch 1, sc in each st across, turn. At end of last row, fasten off.

2ND LEG
Row 4: Sk next 9 unworked sts on row 3, join with sc in next st, sc in each of next 2 sts, turn. *(3 sc)*

Rows 5 & 6: Ch 1, sc in each st across, turn. At end of last row, fasten off.

Rep 2nd Leg twice.

SEAT
Row 7: Working in starting ch on opposite side of row 1, sk first 4 chs, join with sl st in next ch, ch 4, sk next ch, dc in next ch, [ch 1, sk next ch, dc in next ch] across, leaving last 4 chs unworked, turn. *(31 sts and chs)*

Row 8: Ch 1, sc in each st and in each ch across, turn.

Rows 9–19: Ch 1, sc in each st across, turn.

Row 20: Working this row in **back lps** *(see Stitch Guide)*, ch 1, sc in each st across, turn.

Row 21: Rep row 9.

Row 22: **Ch 3** *(counts as hdc and ch-1)*, sk next st, hdc in next st, [ch 1, sk next st, hdc in next st] 3 times, hdc in each of next 2 sts, [ch 1, sk next st, hdc in next st] 5 times, hdc in each of next 2 sts, [ch 1, sk next st, hdc in next st] 4 times, turn.

Rows 23–26: Ch 3, hdc in next st, [ch 1, hdc in next st] 3 times, hdc in each of next 2 sts, [ch 1, hdc in next st] 5 times, hdc in each of next 2 sts, [ch 1, hdc in next st] 4 times, turn. At end of last row, fasten off.

Last row is top.

Leaving bottom edge unsewn, sew sides and top edges of Covering Inside Piece to inside front edge of Sofa.

Tack legs to Bottom of Sofa.

OUTSIDE ARM PIECE
MAKE 2.
Row 1: Ch 16, sc in 2nd ch from hook and in each ch across, turn. *(15 sc)*

FIRST LEG
Row 2: Ch 1, sc in each of first 3 sts leaving rem sts unworked, turn. *(3 sc)*

Rows 3 & 4: Ch 1, sc in each st across, turn. At end of last row, fasten off.

2ND LEG
Row 2: Sk next 9 unworked sts on row 1, join with sc in next st, sc in each of last 2 sts, turn.

Rows 3 & 4: Rep rows 3 and 4 of First Leg.

SIDE

Row 5: Working in starting ch on opposite side of row 1, join with sl st in first ch, ch 4 *(counts first dc and ch-1)*, sk next ch, dc in next ch, [ch 1, sk next ch, dc in next ch] across, turn. *(15 sts and chs)*

Row 6: Ch 1, sc in each st and in each ch across, turn.

Rows 7 & 8: Ch 1, sc in each st across, turn.

Row 9: Ch 4, sk next st, dc in next st, [ch 1, sk next st, dc in next st] across, turn.

Rows 10 & 11: Rep rows 6 and 7.

Row 12: Ch 1, sc in each of first 6 sts, leaving rem sts unworked, turn.

Row 13: Ch 1, sk first st, sc in each st across, turn.

Row 14: Ch 1, sc in each of first 3 sts, sc dec in last 2 sts, turn.

Row 15: Ch 1, sk first st, sc dec in next 2 sts, sc in last st. Fasten off.

Sew Covering Outside Arm Piece to Sofa Outside Arm, sewing matching edges on Legs tog at front corners and tacking Legs to bottom.

BOTTOM TRIM PIECE

Ch 30 or length needed to fit across row 3 on Inside Piece of Covering, sc in 2nd ch from hook and in each ch across. Fasten off. Glue or tack piece across row 3 on Inside Piece of Covering.

UPPER TRIM PIECE

Row 1: Ch 89 or length needed to fit from bottom of right leg, up over Arm, across the Back and down 2nd Arm to bottom, sc in 2nd ch from hook, sc in each ch across, turn.

Place on Sofa, using scrap piece of yarn, mark 2 sts at each top corner.

Row 2: Ch 3, dc in each st across with 3 dc in each marked corner st, remove markers. Fasten off.

Starting at bottom of right leg, keeping piece as flat as possible, sew or glue Trim up and over Arm, across Back being sure to match corners and down opposite Arm to end of Leg at left bottom.

CHAIR
FRONT

Row 1: Ch 14, sc in 2nd ch from hook and in each ch across, turn. *(13 sc)*

Rows 2–32: Ch 1, sc in each st across, turn. At end of last ro, fasten off.

INSIDE ARM & OUTSIDE ARM

Work same as Inside Arm and Outside Arm pieces of Sofa.

BOTTOM

Row 1: Ch 18, sc in 2nd ch from hook and in each ch across, turn. *(17 sc)*

Row 2: Ch 2, hdc in each st across, turn.

Row 3: Ch 1, sc in each st across, turn.

Rows 4–9: [Rep rows 2 and 3 alternately] 3 times. At end of last row, fasten off.

BACK

Row 1: Ch 16, sc in 2nd ch from hook and in each ch across, turn. *(15 sc)*

Row 2: Ch 2, hdc in each st across, turn.

Row 3: Ch 1, sc in each st across, turn.

Rows 4–14: [Rep rows 2 and 3 alternately] 6 times, ending last rep with row 2. At end of last row, fasten off.

ASSEMBLY

1. From foam board, cut 1 each of the following pieces:

1½ x 3¼ inches for Seat Front

2¼ x 3¼ inches for Seat

2¼ x 3¼ inches for Seat Back

2¾ x 3¼ inches for Bottom

3¾ x 3¼ inches for Back

2. Repeat steps 2–5 of Sofa Assembly.

CHAIR COVERING
INSIDE PIECE
Row 1: Ch 20, sc in 2nd ch from hook and in each ch across, turn. *(19 sc)*

FIRST LEG
Row 2: Ch 1, sc in each of first 4 sts, leaving rem sts unworked, turn. *(4 sc)*

Rows 3 & 4: Ch 1, sc in each st across, turn. At end of last row, fasten off.

2ND LEG
Row 2: Sk next 11 unworked sts on row 1, join with sc in next st, sc in each of last 3 sts, turn.

Rows 3 & 4: Rep rows 3 and 4 of First Leg.

SIDE
Row 5: Working in starting ch on opposite side of row 1, sk first 3 chs, join with sl st in next ch, ch 4 *(counts as first dc and ch-1)*, sk next ch, dc in next ch, [ch 1, sk next ch, dc in next ch] across leaving last 3 chs unworked, turn.

Row 6: Ch 1, sc in each st and in each ch across, turn. *(13 sc)*

Rows 7–19: Ch 1, sc in each st across, turn.

Row 20: Working in back lps, ch 1, sc in each st across, turn.

Row 21: Rep row 7.

Row 22: Ch 3 *(counts first hdc and ch-1)*, sk next st, hdc in next st, [ch 1, sk next st, hdc in next st] across, turn.

Rows 23–26: Ch 3, hdc in next st, [ch 1, hdc in next st] across, turn.

Row 27: Ch 1, sc in each st and in each ch across. Fasten off.

Sew Covering Inside Piece to inside front of Chair. Tack Legs to Bottom of Chair.

OUTSIDE ARM PIECE
MAKE 2.
Work same as Outside Arm Piece of Sofa Covering.

BOTTOM TRIM PIECE

With ch 15, work same as Bottom Trim Piece of Sofa.

UPPER TRIM PIECE

With ch 66, work same as Upper Trim Piece of Sofa.

CUSHION
MAKE 4.
SIDE
MAKE 2.

Row 1: Ch 12, sc in 2nd ch from hook and in each ch across, turn. *(11 sc)*

Rows 2–10: Ch 1, sc in each st across, turn.

Rnd 11: Working around outer edge, ch 1, sc in each st and in end of each row and in each ch in starting ch on opposite side or row 1 around with 2 sc in each corner, join with sl st in beg sc. Fasten off.

With RS of pieces held tog and Sew tog through back lps, stuffing before closing.

Place 3 Cushions in Sofa and 1 Cushion in Chair as shown in photo. ∎

Blue Dress

DESIGN BY **JUANITA TURNER**

SKILL LEVEL

INTERMEDIATE

FINISHED SIZE

Fits 11½-inch fashion doll

MATERIALS

- Size 10 rayon crochet thread: 85 yds blue
- Size 7/1.65mm steel crochet hook or hook needed to obtain gauge
- Sewing needle
- Matching sewing thread
- Small silk flowers: 2
- 3mm strung pearl beads: 6 inches
- Straight pins: 5
- Small snaps: 2
- Craft glue

GAUGE

9 sc = 1 inch; 11 sc rows = 1 inch

PATTERN NOTES

Chain-3 at beginning of row or rounds count as first double crochet unless otherwise stated.

Join with slip stitch as indicated unless otherwise stated.

SPECIAL STITCH

Shell: (3 dc, ch 1, 3 dc) in place indicted.

INSTRUCTIONS

DRESS
BODICE

Row 1: Starting at waist, ch 28, sc in 2nd ch from hook and in each ch across, turn. *(27 sc)*

Rows 2–12: Ch 1, sc in each st across, turn.

Rows 13 & 14: Ch 1, **sc dec** (see Stitch Guide) in first 2 sts, sc in each st across to last 2 sts, sc dec in last 2 sts, turn. (23 sc at end of last row)

Row 15: Ch 1, sc dec in first 2 sts, sc in each of next 2 sts, sk next st, 2 dc in each of next 5 sts, sk next st, sc in next st, sk next st, 2 dc in each of next 5 sts, sk next st, sc in each of next 2 sts, sc dec in last 2 sts, turn. (27 sts)

Row 16: Ch 1, sc dec in first 2 sts, sc in next st, sk next st, dc in each of next 8 sts, sk next st, sc in next st, sk next st, dc in each of next 8 sts, sk next st, sc in next st, sc dec in last 2 sts, turn. (21 sts)

Row 17: Ch 1, sc dec in first 2 sts, hdc in next st, dc in each of next 5 sts, sk next st, sc in next st, sk next st, dc in each of next 5 sts, hdc in next st, sc in next st, sc dec in last 2 sts, turn. (17 sts)

Row 18: Ch 1, sc in each of first 8 sts, sc in next worked st on row 14 (to form dip at center front of Bodice), sc in each st across. Fasten off.

STRAPS
Row 1: Working in ends of rows on Bodice, join with sc in end of row 1, evenly sp 17 sc across ends of rows, ch 15, turn. (18 sc, 15 chs)

Row 2: Sc in 2nd ch from hook and in each ch and in each st across. Fasten off.

Rep in ends of rows on opposite side of Bodice.

SKIRT
Row 1: Working in ends of rows on Straps, join with sc in end of first row, sc in next row, working in starting ch on opposite side of row 1 on Bodice, sc in each ch across, sc in end of each row on 2nd Strap, turn. (31 sc)

Row 2: Ch 1, sc in each of first 2 sts, 2 sc in next st, [sc in each of next 2 sts, 2 sc in next st] across to last st, sc in last st, turn. (41 sc)

Row 3: Ch 3 (see Pattern Notes), 2 dc in same st, sk next st, sc in next st, sk next st, *shell (see Special Stitch) in next st, sk next st, sc in next st, sk next st, rep from * across to last st, 3 dc in last st, turn. (6 dc, 9 shells, 10 sc)

Row 4: Ch 1, sc in first st, shell in next sc, [sc in ch sp of next shell, shell in next sc] across, sc in last st, turn. (10 shells)

Row 5: Ch 3, 2 dc in same st, sc in ch sp next shell, [shell in next sc, sc in ch sp of next shell] across, 3 dc in last st, turn.

Rows 6–8: [Rep rows 4 and 5 alternately] twice, ending last rep with row 4.

Rnd 9: Now working in rnds, ch 3, 2 dc in same st, sc in ch sp of next shell, [shell in next sc, sc in ch sp of next shell] around, 3 dc in last st, **join** (see Pattern Notes) in 3rd ch of beg ch-3.

Rnd 10: Ch 1, sc in first st, shell in next sc, [sc in ch sp of next shell, shell in next sc] around, join in beg sc.

Rnd 11: Ch 3, (2 dc, ch 1, 3 dc) in same st, sc in ch sp of next shell, [shell in next sc, sc in ch sp of next shell] around, join in 3rd ch of beg ch-3.

Rnd 12: Sl st in each st across to ch-1 sp, (sl st, ch 1, sc) in ch sp, [shell in next sc, sc in ch sp of next shell] around, join in beg sc.

Rnds 13–18: [Rep rnds 11 and 12 alternately] 3 times. At end of last rnd, fasten off.

FINISHING
Sew 1 snap to back of Dress.

Sew 2 holes only on half of 1 snap to 1 end of neck strap (will overlap the end), sew all 4 holes on 2nd half of snap to opposite end of neck strap.

Cut strung pearls in half. Fold each piece in half and glue 1 to back of each flower.

Glue 1 flower to waistline of Dress.

Style hair and pin flower in place as desired. ∎

Red Dress

DESIGN BY **JUANITA TURNER**

SKILL LEVEL

INTERMEDIATE

FINISHED SIZE
Fits 11½-inch fashion doll

MATERIALS
- Size 10 rayon crochet thread:
    125 yds red
- Size 7/1.65mm steel crochet hook
  or hook needed to obtain gauge
- Sewing needle
- Red sewing thread
- Large gold ribbon rose
- Straight pin
- Small snaps: 4

GAUGE
9 sc = 1 inch; 11 sc rows = 1 inch

PATTERN NOTES
Chain-3 at beginning of row or round counts as
  first double crochet unless otherwise stated.

Join with slip stitch as indicated unless
  otherwise stated.

INSTRUCTIONS
DRESS
BODICE
Row 1: Starting at waist, ch 29, sc in 2nd ch from
  hook and in each ch across, turn. (*28 sc*)

Rows 2 & 3: Ch 1, sc in each st across, turn.

Row 4: Ch 1, sc in each of first 10 sts, 2 sc in each
  of next 2 sts, sc in each of next 4 sts, 2 sc in each
  of next 2 sts, sc in each of last 10 sts, turn. (*32 sc*)

Row 5: Ch 1, sc in each of first 10 sts, 2 sc in
  each of next 2 sts, sc in each of next 8 sts, 2 sc
  in each of next 2 sts, sc in each of last 10 sts,
  turn. (*36 sc*)

Row 6: Ch 1, sc in each st across, turn.

Row 7: Ch 1, sc in each of first 10 sts, 2 sc in each
  of next 2 sts, sc in each of next 12 sts, 2 sc in
  each of next 2 sts, sc in each of last 10 sts, turn.
  (*40 sc*)

Row 8: Ch 1, sc in each of first 10 sts, 2 sc in
  each of next 2 sts, sc in each of next 16 sts, 2
  sc in each of next 2 sts, sc in each of last 10 sts,
  turn. (*44 sc*)

Rows 9–13: Ch 1, sc in each st across, turn.

Row 14: Ch 1, sc in each of first 18 sts, 2 sc in each of next 8 sts, sc in each of last 18 sts, turn. *(52 sc)*

Rows 15–17: Ch 1, sc in each st across, turn.

Row 18: Ch 1, sc in each of first 17 sts, [**sc dec** *(see Stitch Guide)* in next 2 sts, sc in each of next 6 sts] twice, sc dec in next 2 sts, sc in each of last 17 sts, turn. *(49 sc)*

Row 19: Ch 1, sc in each of first 16 sts, sc dec in next 2 sts, sc in each of next 6 sts, sc in next worked sc of row 15 *(to form dip at center front)*, sk st behind sc just made, sc in each of next 6 sts, sc dec in next 2 sts, sc in each of last 16 sts, turn.

Row 20: Ch 1, sl st in each of first 17 sts, sc in each of next 6 sts, sl st in next st, sc in each of next 6 sts, sl st in each st across. Fasten off.

SKIRT
Row 1: Working in starting ch on opposite side of row 1 on Bodice, join with sc in first ch, sc in same ch, 2 sc in each ch across, turn. *(56 sc)*

Row 2: Ch 3 *(see Pattern Notes)*, 2 dc in **back lp** *(see Stitch Guide)* of same st as ch-3, [dc in **front lp** *(see Stitch Guide)* of next st, 2 dc in back lp of same st] across, turn. *(168 dc)*

Row 3: Ch 1, sc in each st across, turn.

Row 4: Ch 3, dc in each st across, turn.

Rows 5–9: [Rep rows 3 and 4 alternately] 3 times, ending last rep with row 3.

Rnd 10: Now working in rnds, ch 3, dc in each st around, **join** *(see Pattern Notes)* in 3rd ch of beg ch-3, turn.

Rnd 11: Ch 1, sc in each st around, join in beg sc, turn.

Rnds 12–19: [Rep rnds 10 and 11 alternately] 4 times. At end of last rnd, fasten off.

Sew snaps evenly spaced down back opening of Dress.

BOW TIE
Row 1: Ch 9, sc in 2nd ch from hook and in each ch across, turn. *(8 sc)*

Rows 2 & 3: Ch 1, sc in each st across, turn. At end of last row, fasten off.

Cut 6-inch length of rayon and wrap tightly around center of Bow Tie, secure end.

NECK STRAP
Ch 17, sc in 2nd ch from hook, sc in each ch across. Fasten off.

Sew 2 holes only on half of 1 snap to 1 end of Neck Strap *(will overlap the end)*, sew all 4 holes on 2nd half of snap to opposite end of Neck Strap.

Sew Bow Tie to center of Neck Strap.

FINISHIING
Style hair and pin ribbon rose in place as desired. ∎

Black Dress

DESIGN BY **JUANITA TURNER**

SKILL LEVEL

INTERMEDIATE

FINISHED SIZE
Fits 11½-inch fashion doll

MATERIALS
- Size 10 metallic crochet thread:
    125 yds black
    10 yds white
- Size 7/1.65mm steel crochet hook
  or hook needed to obtain gauge
- Sewing needle
- Black sewing thread
- Large red carnation
- Straight pin
- Small snaps: 4

GAUGE
9 sc = 1 inch; 11 sc rows = 1 inch

PATTERN NOTES
Chain-3 at beginning of row or round counts as
  first double crochet unless otherwise stated.

Join with slip stitch as indicated unless
  otherwise stated.

INSTRUCTIONS
DRESS
BODICE
Row 1: Starting at waist, with black, ch 27, sc in 2nd
ch from hook and in each ch across, turn. (*26 sc*)

Rows 2 & 3: Ch 1, sc in each st across, turn.

Row 4: Ch 1, sc in each of first 9 sts, 2 sc in each of next 2 sts, sc in each of next 4 sts, 2 sc in each of next 2 sts, sc in each of last 9 sts, turn. *(30 sc)*

Row 5: Ch 1, sc in each of first 10 sts, 2 sc in each of next 2 sts, sc in each of next 6 sts, 2 sc in each of next 2 sts, sc in each of last 10 sts, turn. *(34 sc)*

Row 6: Ch 1, sc in each st across, turn.

Row 7: Ch 1, sc in each of first 10 sts, [2 sc in each of next 2 sts, sc in each of next 10 sts] twice, turn. *(38 sc)*

Row 8: Ch 1, sc in each of first 10 sts, 2 sc in each of next 2 sts, sc in each of next 14 sts, 2 sc in each of next 2 sts, sc in each of last 10 sts, turn. *(42 sc)*

Rows 9 & 10: Ch 1, sc in each st across, turn.

Row 11: Ch 1, sc in each of first 12 sts, 2 sc in next st, sc in each of next 16 sts, 2 sc in next st, sc in each of last 12 sts, turn. *(44 sc)*

Row 12: Ch 1, sc in each of first 18 sts, 2 sc in each of next 8 sts, sc in each of last 18 sts, turn. *(52 sc)*

Rows 13–15: Ch 1, sc in each st across, turn.

Row 16: Ch 1, sc in each of first 7 sts, ch 14, sk next 8 sts *(armhole)*, sc in each of next 22 sts, ch 14, sk next 8 sts *(armhole)*, sc in each st across, turn. *(36 sc, 28 chs)*

Row 17: Ch 1, sc in each of first 6 sts, sk next st, sc in each of next 14 chs, sk next st, sc in each of next 8 sts, sk next st, sc dec in next 2 sts, sk next st, sc in each of next 8 sts, sk next st, sc in each of next 14 chs, sk next st, sc in each st across. Fasten off.

SKIRT

Row 1: Working in starting ch on opposite side of row 1 on Bodice, join black with sc in first ch, sc in each ch across, turn. *(26 sc)*

Row 2: Ch 1, sc in each of first 3 sts, 2 sc in each of next 8 sts, sc in each of next 4 sts, 2 sc in each of next 8 sts, sc in each of last 3 sts, turn. *(42 sc)*

Rows 3–5: Ch 1, sc in each st across, turn.

Row 6: Ch 1, sc in each of first 10 sts, 2 sc in each of next 2 sts, sc in each of next 18 sts, 2 sc in each of next 2 sts, sc in each of last 10 sts, turn. *(46 sc)*

Rows 7–12: Ch 1, sc in each st across, turn.

Rnds 13–15: Now working in rnds, ch 1, sc in each st around, **join** *(see Pattern Notes)* in beg sc, **turn.**

Rnd 16: Ch 1, sc in each of first 10 sts, 2 sc in next st, sc in each of next 24 sts, 2 sc in next st, sc in each of last 10 sts, join in beg sc, turn. *(48 sc)*

Rnds 17–21: Ch 1, sc in each st around, join in beg sc, turn.

Rnd 22: Ch 1, sc in each of first 10 sts, 2 sc in next st, sc in each of next 26 sts, 2 sc in next st, sc in each of last 10 sts, join in beg sc, turn. *(50 sc)*

Rnds 23–27: Ch 1, sc in each st around, join in beg sc, turn.

Rnd 28: Ch 1, sc in each of first 10 sts, 2 sc in next st, sc in each of next 28 sts, 2 sc in next st, sc in each of last 10 sts, join in beg sc, turn. *(52 sc)*

Rnds 29–33: Ch 1, sc in each st around, join in beg sc, turn.

Rnd 34: Ch 1, sc in each of first 10 sts, 2 sc in next st, sc in each of next 30 sts, 2 sc in next st, sc in each of last 10 sts, join in beg sc, turn. *(54 sc)*

Rnds 35–39: Ch 1, sc in each st around, join in beg sc, turn.

Rnd 40: Ch 1, sc in each of first 10 sts, 2 sc in next st, sc in each of next 32 sts, 2 sc in next st, sc in each of last 10 sts, join in beg sc, turn. *(56 sc)*

Rnds 41–45: Ch 1, sc in each st around, join in beg sc, turn.

Rnd 46: Ch 1, sc in each of first 15 sts, 2 sc in next st, sc in each of next 24 sts, 2 sc in next st, sc in each of last 15 sts, join in beg sc, turn. *(58 sc)*

Rnds 47–64: Ch 1, sc in each st around, join in beg sc, turn. At end of last rnd, fasten off.

Sew snaps evenly sp down back opening of Dress.

TRIM

With white, [ch 4, 2 tr in 4th ch from hook] 33 times. Fasten off.

Starting on right back of Bodice, tack Trim to inside of shoulder strap, at an angle across front of Bodice and down left side and around last rnd of Skirt as shown in photo.

FINISHING

Style hair and pin carnation in place as desired. ■

TOLL-FREE ORDER LINE or to request a free catalog (800) LV-ANNIE (800) 582 6643
Customer Service (800) AT-ANNIE (800) 282-6643, **Fax** (800) 882-6643
Visit AnniesAttic.com

We have made every effort to ensure the accuracy and completeness of these instructions.
We cannot, however, be responsible for human error, typographical mistakes or variations in individual work.

ISBN: 978-1-59635-233-9

Printed in USA   1 2 3 4 5 6 7 8 9

Stitch Guide

For more complete information, visit **FreePatterns.com**

ABBREVIATIONS

beg	begin/begins/beginning
bpdc	back post double crochet
bpsc	back post single crochet
bptr	back post treble crochet
CC	contrasting color
ch(s)	chain(s)
ch-	refers to chain or space previously made (e.g., ch-1 space)
ch sp(s)	chain space(s)
cl(s)	cluster(s)
cm	centimeter(s)
dc	double crochet (singular/plural)
dc dec	double crochet 2 or more stitches together, as indicated
dec	decrease/decreases/decreasing
dtr	double treble crochet
ext	extended
fpdc	front post double crochet
fpsc	front post single crochet
fptr	front post treble crochet
g	gram(s)
hdc	half double crochet
hdc dec	half double crochet 2 or more stitches together, as indicated
inc	increase/increases/increasing
lp(s)	loop(s)
MC	main color
mm	millimeter(s)
oz	ounce(s)
pc	popcorn(s)
rem	remain/remains/remaining
rep(s)	repeat(s)
rnd(s)	round(s)
RS	right side
sc	single crochet (singular/plural)
sc dec	single crochet 2 or more stitches together, as indicated
sk	skip/skipped/skipping
sl st(s)	slip stitch(es)
sp(s)	space(s)/spaced
st(s)	stitch(es)
tog	together
tr	treble crochet
trtr	triple treble
WS	wrong side
yd(s)	yard(s)
yo	yarn over

Chain—ch: Yo, pull through lp on hook.

Slip stitch—sl st: Insert hook in st, pull through both lps on hook.

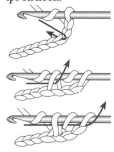

Single crochet—sc: Insert hook in st, yo, pull through st, yo, pull through both lps on hook.

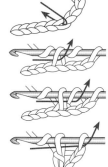

Front post stitch—fp: Back post stitch—bp: When working post st, insert hook from right to left around post st on previous row.

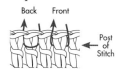

Front loop—front lp Back loop—back lp

Half double crochet—hdc: Yo, insert hook in st, yo, pull through st, yo, pull through all 3 lps on hook.

Double crochet—dc: Yo, insert hook in st, yo, pull through st, [yo, pull through 2 lps] twice.

Change colors: Drop first color; with 2nd color, pull through last 2 lps of st.

Treble crochet—tr: Yo twice, insert hook in st, yo, pull through st, [yo, pull through 2 lps] 3 times.

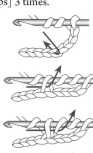

Double treble crochet—dtr: Yo 3 times, insert hook in st, yo, pull through st, [yo, pull through 2 lps] 4 times.

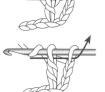

Single crochet decrease (sc dec): (Insert hook, yo, draw lp through) in each of the sts indicated, yo, draw through all lps on hook.

Example of 2-sc dec

Half double crochet decrease (hdc dec): (Yo, insert hook, yo, draw lp through) in each of the sts indicated, yo, draw through all lps on hook.

Example of 2-hdc dec

Double crochet decrease (dc dec): (Yo, insert hook, yo, draw loop through, draw through 2 lps on hook) in each of the sts indicated, yo, draw through all lps on hook.

Example of 2-dc dec

Example of 2-tr dec

Treble crochet decrease (tr dec): Holding back last lp of each st, tr in each of the sts indicated, yo, pull through all lps on hook.

US		UK
sl st (slip stitch)	=	sc (single crochet)
sc (single crochet)	=	dc (double crochet)
hdc (half double crochet)	=	htr (half treble crochet)
dc (double crochet)	=	tr (treble crochet)
tr (treble crochet)	=	dtr (double treble crochet)
dtr (double treble crochet)	=	ttr (triple treble crochet)
skip	=	miss